Samantha Brett is a columnist for the *Sydney Morning Herald*, media personality and Australia's number-one sex, dating and relationships blogger. Her 'Ask Sam' column, which she started in 2006, receives 50,000 hits per day and is one of the most widely read online columns in Australia. Samantha has written for *Grazia*, *Vogue* and *FHM*, appears regularly on *Weekend Sunrise* and gives relationship advice on radio stations across the country. Samantha is the author of *The Chase*.

The
Catch

The Catch

How to be found by the man of your dreams

SAMANTHA BRETT

ARENA
ALLEN&UNWIN

First published in 2012

Copyright © Samantha Brett 2012

Arena Books, an imprint of
Allen & Unwin
Sydney, Melbourne, Auckland, London

83 Alexander Street
Crows Nest NSW 2065
Australia
Phone: (61 2) 8425 0100
Fax: (61 2) 9906 2218
Email: info@allenandunwin.com
Web: www.allenandunwin.com

Cataloguing-in-Publication details are available
from the National Library of Australia
www.trove.nla.gov.au

ISBN 978 1 74237 615 8

Set in 12/16 pt Bembo by Midland Typesetters, Australia
Printed in Australia by McPherson's Printing Group

10 9 8 7 6 5 4 3 2

MIX
Paper from
responsible sources
FSC
www.fsc.org   FSC® C001695

The paper in this book is FSC® certified.
FSC® promotes environmentally responsible,
socially beneficial and economically viable
management of the world's forests.

To all the men I've dated, bedded, wept over, brushed off and confided in over the past year . . . thank you . . . you weren't just case-study material . . . I promise.

Contents

Prologue

If you have just picked up *The Catch*, I want to assure you that your life is about to change . . . for the better. All those feelings of insecurity, of not being able to get the man you want, of not knowing where to find him or what to say once you do—will evaporate pretty quickly after you start doing all the exercises outlined in this book. I'm so excited to introduce you to a brand-new method of living, dating and being that will see you become the woman you were supposed to be, and will see you *instantly* attracting the man you are supposed to be with. No more pining over a man who broke your heart or used you for sex. Instead, you will find, catch and keep a man who will value the true you, exactly where you are in your life right now.

If you've just been dumped, or you've lost a man who you thought had every potential to be the last man you will ever sleep with, or if you have been dating douchebag, after player, after man who disappoints you, this book is for you.

If you truly believed he was the one who was going to propose to you and make all your dreams come true—whether you'd been dating him for a couple of years or only a couple of months—it doesn't matter. We could meet a man once, and we could instantly think that he has all the potential in the world of being the perfect boyfriend, husband and father to our future kids. And then without even knowing we are doing it, we put all our hopes into this dude, and still get heartbroken when we realise he never had the same intentions as us.

Becoming The Catch is all about looking rationally at why you let yourself feel this way, and then never again launching into something that isn't going to be 100 per cent satisfying in the long term. You are going to refine your checklist, never again settle for less, and know how to handle and talk to the man of your dreams then make him fall hopelessly in love with you in no time at all.

When you complete all the exercises in this book, you will find yourself no longer wasting your precious time or energy on men who aren't good enough for you, don't value you like you deserve to be valued, and generally aren't the right man for you. That time of your life is over, kaput, finito! What this means too, though, is that you are going to not only become The Catch—a woman who men flock to get to know—but you're going to become someone who men instantly see as 'girlfriend material'. That means that men will start to have the utmost respect for you; want to provide for and protect you; aren't opposed to waiting for sex with you; are proud to call you 'girlfriend' in front of their mates; and you will feel like your best self whenever you are around them. He likes you for you; he likes everything about you; and he likes you where you are *right now* in your life.

You are going to get into a zone in which you will have more date invitations than you can handle and yet you are now at a wiser, more sensible place in your life, so you can instantly separate the players from the stayers. You will learn to know what you want, and then when the timing is right, it will magically appear in your lap. You are about to morph from someone who has been tossed by men to someone who is viewed as The Catch—a long-term prospect. So let's get started!

Part 1

Welcome to *The Catch*

♥ ♥

A Cautionary Tale: Camilla

There are two types of single women in this world: those men want to marry, and those men just want to fuck. Camilla Mason was the type of woman men wanted to marry right away, the minute they laid eyes on her. A political journalist for a major newspaper, she had cropped blonde hair, a tiny waist and big breasts. She was smart, sexy and aloof. Hence every man she met wanted her . . . to be their girlfriend.

'You're exactly the type of girl I've been looking for,' the men would say. Not that she gave a toss. After all, for the last five years she'd been ensconced in a long-term relationship. Which meant that despite men instantly turning to mush at first sight of her, she was always unavailable. Always busy. Always dismissive.

#1. THE CATCH NEVER CHASES MEN

The Catch has men flocking towards her . . . even though most of the time she's taken anyway. Women who are The Catch never chase men, *they* flock to *her*. Even if she ignores them. *Especially* when she ignores them.

Of course, this hot-to-trot attitude only made the men more desperate to be around Camilla. But she already had a man who she adored. Or at least that's what she told herself. Even though she didn't have a ring—and even though she knew there were issues in their relationship which she preferred to sweep under the carpet—she was mightily happy. After all, who needed marriage when she had a career to focus on? Having a ring, a big wedding and creating a family were the last things on her mind.

Camilla truly believed that her kind, doting boyfriend would always be around . . . even when she upped and travelled to Washington for months on end for her career (without him); even when she flirted with other men (for work purposes in order to get a story); even when she disappeared for days in search of a yarn. Even when she told him she never wanted to get married because, to her, marriage signified death. Or at least the death of her glamorous life. She simply assumed that he'd still be waiting at home for her with bated breath and a soufflé in the oven.

No such luck. The more she pushed her luck, focused on her career, the more he pulled away. Until one day he decided he just couldn't do it any more.

Especially since he'd lost his job in the financial crisis. While Camilla flaunted her career success, her boyfriend began to feel rather useless. It seemed he felt like she didn't need him or rely on him for anything. He hated her newfound lifestyle and with her being away so often, he fell into a deep depression. Suddenly the 'perfect' boyfriend didn't seem so perfect any more.

#2. VALUE YOUR MAN AND MAKE HIM NUMBER ONE

Once you are in a secure, committed relationship, your man should become your top priority. He should always be put first—above your work, your friends, your partying ways. Men are highly sensitive creatures and you've made him work so hard to catch you, the least you can do is prioritise him.

Unfortunately, Camilla had committed the cardinal sin— she'd put her man second. She never stopped to think about his needs, only her own. And when he stayed in bed all too often, sometimes past lunchtime, she never stopped to think why, or how she could help out. Instead the relationship began to die a slow death and, sadly, it felt like there was nothing either of them could do about it. And now, armed with a mini-skirt, heels and an insatiable urge to find a new man—any man—to replace the giant hole in her heart, here she was almost 30 years old, out on the town alone, thrust headfirst into an unknown territory—a treacherous singles scene that required some serious knowledge of martial arts if she ever wanted to get through it alive, without another broken heart, a broken nose or an STD.

'But I thought it was hip to be single!' she lamented to her single girlfriends over bellinis a few months after her Big Break-up. It was her 28th birthday and all her girlfriends had gathered to celebrate. It was the first birthday she'd had since

she was 18 that a boyfriend wasn't there. Or any man that was interested in her for that matter.

#3. A MAN NEEDS TO FEEL NEEDED

When a man feels as though he is not 'needed' by a woman, he feels like he has no purpose being in a relationship with her. This is why so many men prefer to date their secretaries rather than their bosses. Women who need men are more sought after as, biologically, a man's manhood is founded on his ability to provide and protect for a woman. But there's a difference between a woman who needs a man, and being needy.

'I'm 28, single, and there's not a man in sight. How did this happen to me?'

She was complaining to the same girls who had all encouraged her to dump her man in order to pursue her journalistic dreams and to 'see what else is out there'. But she realised that they hadn't exactly been honest with her. Being single was a nightmare; the available men around were even worse.

'I thought it was so easy being single, so much fun, filled with cocktails and glam times. No-one warned me of this. How much more of it am I supposed to be able to handle?' By 'this', she was referring to the neverending cycle of men who

continually disappointed her. Who lied, were dating multiple women at once (unbeknown to her), who led her on, and used her for sex. God, was it really this hard?

#4. YOUR EX IS NOT THE ANSWER

When you find yourself stuck on a merry-go-round of bad dates with bad men, do not think that your ex might be the ultimate solution to your loneliness. He is not. You broke up for a reason (or multiple reasons) so don't forget that, despite the treacherous dating scene, you are definitely better off single than you are getting back with your ex. Grovelling back when you are at this vulnerable stage of your life will not accomplish anything. He is not your fall-back guy. Your fall-back position is about to revealed in the pages of this book. When you are ready to meet the man of your dreams, you will. Everyone goes through the ups and downs of the dating process—it's the only way you learn. So try and enjoy it. And as clichéd as it may sound, try and see it as a journey, not a destination.

She had no problem meeting men. But the men she did meet were all the same. None of them wanted to commit any time soon, or at least not to her. And suddenly she realised that what she'd had was rather special. And she'd royally fucked it up to the point of no return.

The Catch

After months of being tossed around in the tough dating cycle, she found herself lying awake on Kate's couch, wishing and praying to be back in the arms of her Mr Ex. Sure, he hadn't supported her dreams, he'd put her down and he hadn't liked her friends, but he was safe, secure, real. *Would there ever be anyone better out there? Could anyone else ever really love her like he had? Was this the biggest mistake of her life?*

1

The Catch

The Catch (n.): The Catch is—according to the men I've polled—the ultimate female prize. She is the woman every man wants to date, make his girl-friend, marry and make happy for the rest of her life. The Catch has a different mindset. And it is the way you need to view yourself whether you're in a rela-tionship or single. It doesn't matter. But above all, The Catch knows her value and what she'll accept when it comes to men. And she'll accept nothing less than the best.

Catch versus Toss

The Toss (n.): The Toss is the woman who—for no reason other than she hasn't wisened up to the dating game—is constantly tossed back after a man has his way with her. She looks no different to The Catch, but it's all about her attitude, which is needy, desperate, clingy and uncool—a mighty turn-off to men. She accepts their scraps, takes whatever they will dish out, communicates with him too often and doesn't quite understand how the male mind works. If this sounds familiar, read on!

We've all been in the position Camilla currently finds herself in. She's newly single, unaware of the dating rules and desperate to get back into the game as quickly and as seamlessly as possible. Unfortunately it's not that easy. She's on the rebound. She hasn't been alone . . . *ever*. She doesn't know what it means to stand on her own two feet without a man. And she doesn't want to either. She wants to get married, or at least get a boyfriend, as soon as possible. And so she begins to give every potential man she spots the Desperate Eyes.

Why you want to become The Catch

Admit it, you want to be seen as the ultimate Catch. You no longer want to be tossed aside by men after a few dates, a one-night stand or a few months of casual sex. You don't want to be strung along by your boyfriend forever either, with him promising that one day he'll commit to you, only for you to realise years later that it's never going to happen.

Instead, you know you are ready and you want men to see it too. You want them to see you as girlfriend/ wife material. You want men to want to commit to you, to ask you to be their girlfriend, to propose when the time is right, to cherish, love and value you and think he's hit the jackpot just for being in your presence. And yet you're stuck in a world where you so desperately want a partner, yet a football team of men always seem to be chasing after another woman, not you. You sit on the sidelines as you wonder what the heck she has that you don't. Is it bigger breasts? Better hair? Tighter abs? Not exactly.

So let's take a look at exactly who The Catch is, and in subsequent chapters we'll talk about exactly how you can become her.

The characteristics of The Catch

- She is the sexy, fun, funny, charming woman every man wants to chase and get her to commit to *him*.
- She is cool, calm and classy; she isn't demanding or needy. She's smart and ambitious and she's mightily fun to be around.
- Men flock to catch her, but she doesn't let them until they prove they are worthy of her.
- She doesn't try to impress men, but lets them impress her.

- She doesn't let men weigh her down nor does she constantly think about why they haven't texted or wonder about the reasons behind their actions. 'They're just boys!' she says.
- She always has many men chasing her and chooses one based on how much he's willing to prove to her that he's worthy.
- She is always polite, happy, breezy and pleasant in a man's company. That's because she's genuinely having fun. But she doesn't give too much of herself away to them either.
- She is not a drama queen.
- She never waits around for a man to call her and she always has other plans.
- After a man texts or calls her, she usually deletes his number (unless they have plans). This enables her to rid him from her mind until he contacts her again. Only when he asks her to be exclusive with him does she then keep his number in her phone. And even then, she hardly ever uses it.
- Because she's not waiting around for a man to call her and never texts or calls men first, there is room in her life for new men to constantly ask her out.
- The Catch has so many options that she will never make the wrong decision about men. She carefully ascertains whether they will step it up for her and whether they like her enough (and show it—not just say it) in order for her to even fathom giving them a go.

- The Catch never sleeps with a man she doesn't want to, but she doesn't beat herself up over slipping either. She dusts herself off if she makes a mistake and starts The Catch program all over again the minute she does. Because she's a Catch, and she never has to apologise for anything she does. She owns her own decisions and never feels guilty for acting on them!

From the Male Room

'The difference between a girl I want to sleep with and a girl I want to have a relationship with is that the one I want to make my girlfriend makes me feel irrational. I don't act or think reasonably around her. She does something to me that is indescribable. But I think it boils down to her innate knowledge that she is a Catch.'—**Josh**

How men think—and why The Catch theory works

Before we talk about exactly how you can become The Catch, it's important you understand what goes on in the male mind and why, biologically, The Catch holds the power when it comes to nabbing a man. Men are pretty straightforward creatures. They're darn easy to understand and to work out if you just let go of all your expectations and attempts to impress them. Because the truth is that men are hardwired to impress women. And they'll do it over and over again if you let them, say thank you and do nothing in return. That's right— the minute you attempt to 'give' to a man, he suddenly thinks that he's done enough to make you happy and he simply stops trying. Unfortunately it's our natural instincts as women to want to give, give and give— especially to a man who you fancy. But when you do too many things for a man too early on, in his head he thinks he's done enough for you. He doesn't think that he has to do anything any more in return as he feels as though he has already earned you. Sometimes some men will stop trying altogether! The key here is to allow a man to give to you without feeling obligated to return the favour. A simple thank you is enough for a man and it will make him want to continue giving to you more and more. Try it, I dare you.

What The Catch looks like

Contrary to popular belief, The Catch doesn't look like Gisele Bündchen, sport a body like Halle Berry or have the breasts of Heidi Klum. The Catch doesn't dress sluttily either. In fact, often when I see a Catch on the arm of a man who is equally as much of a Catch as she is, I usually stop and note what she looks like. And nine times out of ten, the Catch actually *looks* like a girlfriend. By that I mean she looks content, classy, like she isn't trying too hard. And she *never* looks desperate.

From the Male Room

'When I see a woman who is wearing a tight dress and has her tits hanging out, I usually think that she probably doesn't have much else to offer. When I'm looking for a girlfriend, I'm looking for more than just a dessert handed to me on a platter.'—**Brett**

'The Catch is a woman who is worth keeping. That's not easy to define. In simple terms, would I be ashamed to turn up to my thirty-year high school reunion with this woman, or not?'—**Barry**

The classic Catch

I have a friend, Anna, who is the ultimate Single Catch. She's young and doesn't want a boyfriend at this stage in her life. She's enjoying the male attention she's receiving and she has a neverending list of male suitors lining up to do things for her. She receives flowers, extravagant date invitations, weekends away, even marriage proposals. And here's a word about Anna: whenever I spot her out, she is always dressed in a way that is cool and classy, not slutty or try-hard. She wears skinny jeans, boots, white T-shirts and cool jackets. She wears medium-length skirts to nightclubs teamed with a loose T-shirt or an oversized jumper. Her hair is not over-dyed, but instead a little messy in that cute I-haven't-tried-too-hard way. She is the antithesis of every other woman at the bar wearing dresses that are too tight, heels that are too high and make-up too thick. In essence, Anna looks like a woman who men would want to take home to their mothers; these others are not.

The Pippa Middleton effect

I liken Anna to Pippa Middleton and the effect that her sexy but demure presentation at the royal wedding had over men worldwide. When Kate Middleton's sister walked down the aisle in a slim-line cowl-necked ivory dress with a cinched-in waist and a hint of cleavage, red-blooded males the world over dropped their jaws. Blokes went googly-eyed for the younger sibling of the duchess-to-be and swooned over her on Twitter, Facebook and fan pages alike. The common consensus was simply this: she was hot, hot, hot stuff.

Never before in my work had I seen such a flurry of male interest in a woman on television. Sure, when Sophie Monk first appeared, all bleached-blonde hair and big breasts, on our screens, men didn't talk about much else; or when Pamela Anderson sloshed around Los Angeles's waters in a red one-piece that left little to the imagination, men certainly created new fantasies in their heads. But with Pippa's appearance, it created a new definition of hot and what constitutes a Catch.

Not exactly quite sure what the big appeal actually was, I decided to do a poll of twenty men—some married, some dating but most single. The consensus?

That she's a gal who looks like someone they could take home to their mum.

Of course the jury is still out on how men want a woman they're dating to look. One man I hung out with liked me in flats, T-shirts, my hair pulled back and with minimal make-up. Another preferred mini-skirts, high heels, ample cleavage and long, loosely curled hair.

But as I mentioned before, women who have boyfriends *look like* girlfriends. Look around on a Sunday morning over brunch and you'll notice that the girlfriends are dressed very differently to the single girls. Girlfriends are usually in ballet flats sans make-up, with their hair pulled back. Girlfriends are content, don't look like they're trying too hard and are generally adept at keeping their man's attention without looking like a dessert on a platter. And there is no reason the Single Catch shouldn't dress exactly like she is girlfriend material too. Just like they say you should be dressing for the job you want to get, not the job you have, the same goes for the way you dress when you want to be a girlfriend.

Think about the gaggle of single girls who seem to all be in short skirts and too much make-up. Do they do it to boost their own egos? In the hope of attracting a husband? To increase the amount of male attention directed towards them? Perhaps. But it just doesn't work for them. And the longer they keep to this mindset, the harder pressed they're going to be when it comes to finding a man.

True, some men like fake breasts, others like them natural. Some like long, bleached-blonde hair, others like natural brunettes. Some like their girlfriends to dress demurely; others revel in the fact that every man stops to gawk at their girlfriend as she walks down the street.

But Scott Haltzman, the author of *The Secrets of Happily Married Women*, wrote in his book: 'When a man is in love, what he finds really attractive is the feeling that he's seeing you for who you truly are . . . To a guy, the make-up, the sexy outfit, it's all a mask. He wants the woman behind the mask. Openness, vulnerability, an air of contentment—those things are what really turn him on.'[1]

Nevertheless, I decided to poll three men in depth: a single guy, a boyfriend and a married man. Here's what they had to say:

From the Male Room

The single guy

'The Catch is a healthy, fun, confident, self-respecting girl who is conscious of the way she presents herself. I didn't watch the royal wedding, but I did notice the fan page dedicated to Pippa [on Facebook]! The photos selected on the fan page made it obvious to me why many consider her hot. She has an amazing smile, great figure, she's curvaceous, she's well dressed, poised and elegant yet has an approachable and nurturing vibe. She

would definitely fall into the hot, take home, introduce to the family category and would be popular for the qualities listed above. The difference between a single girl I want to date and one I don't is simple. Short skirts and cleavage bring out the natural instincts in a guy to look at her—after all, it is demanding attention! Some act on that notion and go for a girl who dresses that way. But different guys have different opinions as to whether she's girlfriend material and I personally don't see her as girlfriend material. Instead, the most important thing to me has always been a nice smile. A woman has to be comfortable in what she wears. Nice fashion sense— not necessarily designer labels, but elegant, sophisticated yet cool. Poised and confident in her own skin. Mini- skirts and cleavage have a stigma in this context, but if you can pull it off with the other qualities, why not? Generally though, jeans and a T-shirt work best for me. When it comes to make-up, less is more! Nothing beats the natural look. In terms of celebrities, I like Rachel McAdams, Amy Smart, Natalie Portman. They all have amazing smiles, and a graceful and elegant vibe that shows in the way they carry themselves as well as the way they present themselves.'—**Chad**

The boyfriend

'The Catch oozes confidence, some sort of intelligence, and is physically attractive, i.e. nice body, some curves/ breasts, cute arse, nice skin. She should be well dressed and have class. Pippa Middleton has a beautiful smile,

she's well groomed and she's wholesome. She looks like a girl you could take home to your mum.

'I think the ideal girlfriend wears a short skirt, has nice boobs, nice legs (but all class); is independent, capable and confident; intelligent; successful; faithful; kinky in the bedroom; willing to party and have fun but also enjoy a night in. Plus a girl you want to spend all your hard-earned money on but who doesn't expect *you to. It's also someone who takes pride in herself, someone I can comfortably introduce to friends, family and work colleagues. Also, confidence and a sense of humour help. The physical attributes are hard to nail down—I don't seem to have a certain type that I look for but a healthy, natural look always seems to work.'*—**Michael**

The married guy

'The Catch starts with a pretty face, is augmented by a great figure (for me it's curves rather than skinny or athletic). The package is completed with an intelligent and confident personality. A girl can be hot with the face and figure, but a vacuous or nasty personality rapidly reduces hotness. Similarly a sensational personality increases the attractiveness of a nice face and figure, but a woman really needs a combination of all three to be The Catch.

'My wife doesn't dress "down" and I wouldn't want her to. She's extremely sexy and I know that guys are going to check her out. I don't mind this

because I know she's loyal to me, so I encourage her to wear bikinis at the beach, hot pants when shopping, and tight-fitting dresses on formal occasions. Classy sexy is very different to trampy sexy. I wouldn't want trampy sexy whether single or married. I get a buzz knowing that other guys check out my wife, but that they recognise her as classy sexy rather than trampy sexy. It's a reflection on me that I have such a hot girl on my arm, but what really tops it off is that I know she is an ideal "politician's wife". Whether we're having dinner with a magistrate or mingling with the mayor at a work function, she's an excellent conversationalist who can speak about a range of issues relevant to the nature of the event.

'When my wife was younger she sometimes went a bit overboard with make-up and trying to outdo other girls with skimpy clothes but having matured into an intelligent and classy woman she now knows she doesn't need to compete. She's found her niche and knows how to maximise her style. She's light on the make-up, which I like. When a "Saturday night" event is coming up (wedding, race day, etc.) she'll spend weeks finding the right outfit and always seems to nail the right combination of style and sexiness.

'I like miniskirts and cleavage. Not so much heels. But a "hot" girl makes jeans and T-shirt look good. What I don't like are clothes that are bulky and detract from the girl. Belts, scarves, jewellery, etc. should be minimalist. I don't want to be looking at an *oversized belt when I'd rather be admiring the gentle curve of a hip. I don't want to have five dangling hoop earrings obscuring the sensual slope of a neck. Scarlett Johansson is probably my ideal in terms of hotness and not surprisingly my wife is fairly spot-on in that area with a gorgeous face, long blonde hair, and a curvy figure.'*—**Troy**

All these men are describing their version of what a Catch looks like. And the interesting part is that they all used the word 'classy' in their descriptions. The Catch is cool, not demanding or needy, she's smart and ambitious, and she's mightily fun to be around.

She'll drop men around her at the first sign that they don't live up to her standards, unlike most women, who actually hang around hoping that one day he might just step it up. Oh no. The Catch has way too many men texting and contacting her on a constant basis to worry about the one who isn't. She's not into 'settling', accepting his bullshit, or sleeping with him too soon in fear he'll drop her if she doesn't.

She doesn't have to impress him. In fact, it works the other way around. He's the one clamouring to impress her.

Certainly women's magazines would have us believe that we need to impress a man, wear a sexy black dress on the first date and ask him intelligent questions while regaling him with our achievements. Then we're supposed to accept his dates (no matter how awful), politely answer his text messages (no matter how awful) and jump between the sheets while giving him the best blow job of his life (no matter if he doesn't please you first!). But guess what? The Catch has a different mindset. She is waiting to be caught by the *right man*. Now, how satisfying does all this sound? Not exactly like the terse dating game you're used to, I bet!

From the Male Room

'This is how it works when I meet a girl worthy of my attention. I meet a girl at the bar. I offer her a drink. She looks at me, smiles and says thanks, but she says that she can pay for it herself. She orders a beer. Just like I do. She isn't impressed by the charms that usually make women fall all over me. So I try harder. She doesn't laugh too hard at my jokes. So I make another one. I ask her if she is hungry. She says she is. I take her to a late-night café. She orders a burger. I am impressed. I ask for her number. She gives it to me. I'm eager to text her the following day. She doesn't reply. When I call her the following day, she says she was busy. I ask her to dinner. She is busy till Friday. Damn. I look forward to it all week. She arrives looking hot, but not like she's offering herself up on a platter. I can't really seem to see her cleavage. Just a hint of skin, but she's proving that she isn't easy. I like the challenge. I feel chemistry. I feel sexually charged. I figure out I'll need at least a few dates

before I can try and sleep with her. But I don't want to rush things either. This girl is cool. She suggests we go dancing after dinner. She is fun. She seems low maintenance. Her hair is pulled back in a ponytail. Her heels aren't too high. She isn't wearing fake tan. I want her to be my girlfriend. Heck, I'm starting to think about how I can get her to commit to me. I like her because she's presenting herself as something worth chasing . . . And men are born to hunt and chase until they can catch the ultimate girl. And she's so freaking hard to catch that I can't think about much else other than how I'm going to do it. My booty call buddy sends me a text. I ignore it. I don't want to waste time any more with those floosies. I want a real girl. Like this one. Finally, a woman worthy of my time.'—**Dan**

It's imperative that the single girl presents herself correctly to the world. It's very easy for single women to fall into the 'I-need-to-show-off-my-assets-in-order-to-get-a-guy' mode. Skirts get shorter, T-shirts get tighter, heels get higher, make-up gets thicker, hair gets straighter. A potential Catch can instantly turn herself into a Toss. Men don't take her seriously, and the ones who approach her in the bar are the ones who are only looking for one thing. And when she revels in the attention they serve up to her, she gets herself caught up in a cycle of dating douchebags, who only want casual sex, nothing more.

My girlfriend, Cathy, is another ultimate single Catch. She has men flocking at her feet. Even when she doesn't open her mouth, they clamour to get to know her. And if they can't get anywhere near her (which they usually can't since there is already a group of hot guys surrounding her), then they come up to me and they ask me about her. 'How do you know Cathy?' they say. 'Is she single?'

I often wonder what it is about Cathy that the men are drawn to. Let's talk about how she projects herself as the ultimate single Catch. When I probed the men as to what it is about her that they were drawn to (even before they spoke to her), one response was this: 'She just looks cool. She stands there like she owns the room, but she is quiet in her knowing. She isn't loud or trying to please anyone. She's just smiling, happy and content.'

I know Cathy well and, yes, she's all of these things. But how men pick it on first glance is amazing to me. And so I asked Cathy her secret. And she told me: 'Whenever I'm out I just don't think about guys. I don't even think about myself. I am just in the moment enjoying my time wherever I am. I try to notice things in the room around me, and try not to get caught up in superficial conversations. I'd rather stand on my own than be locked into a conversation I'm not interested in. That way I'm never bored.'

Cathy knows that the secret to being a good single Catch is also in the way she dresses. Which is never over-the-top, never too girly, never too trendy and never looking like she's 'high maintenance'. In fact, she's one of those girls who always wears her hair in a ponytail, and dresses in T-shirts with capped sleeves, miniskirts or leggings, boots and a cute scarf in a neutral tone. She doesn't wear too much make-up either, nor does she carry the latest designer handbag (or if she does, it doesn't have a label on it).

The Cameron Diaz theory

I like to compare Cathy's attitude to that of Cameron Diaz. Cameron Diaz is a single woman, yet when you think about her, you would never think about her as a desperate singleton who is needy or incomplete without a man. Oh no. You think of Cameron as the ultimate sex symbol, comfortable in her own skin and constantly with a gaggle of males (hot males, at that!) around her, all vying for her attention. She has to do absolutely nothing but smile and look pretty. Sure, she takes care of herself and is always spotted exercising, but that's all part of where that innate attitude stems from. Doing things to empower yourself gives you that inner strength that you can then emanate in sticky situations.

When I was single and I had to attend a function on my own—whether it be a wedding, an engagement party, a family dinner—and I knew I would be constantly questioned about why I was single and what was wrong with me, I always envisioned myself as having the

Cameron Diaz attitude. Can you imagine some distant relative asking Cameron Diaz why she wasn't married and what was wrong with her? She would look at them, laugh, tell them to get a life and then dance on her own in the middle of the room to Beyoncé, looking hot, sexy and in control as she was doing it. Cameron could be married, living in the suburbs with two-point-five kids in tow and have conformed to society's expectations of where a 30-something woman should be in her life. Instead, she is a woman of the world who lives life to the max and looks hot, strong and in control while doing it. In other words, Cameron has broken the mould and isn't afraid to be proud about it.

So, whenever you're feeling like you're a loser because you're single or you haven't conformed to society's expectations about where you should be in your life at this point, ask yourself, 'What would Cameron Diaz do?' And then channel your inner Charlie's Angel. It works wonders.

Let's get back to Cathy for a minute. Here's the other thing about her: she's sweet, but she's not a walk-over. And she definitely plays by some stringent dating rules. While I'm not advocating playing games, Cathy always tells me about the fact that she's never sitting at home eagerly waiting for a guy to text or call her . . . ever. In fact, she barely contacts men and she certainly never sleeps with them too soon. Which, contrary to popular thought, actually aids her in oozing a heck of a lot of sexual attractiveness. But her actions are all highly calculated. I used to think that women like Cathy just had the knack for being naturally extremely brilliant with men. But as I probed Cathy more and more, I began to realise that everything she was doing was extremely counter-intuitive.

Because of her dating prowess, just like Cameron Diaz, Cathy is never embarrassed to be single. But here's the caveat: the men Cathy actually chooses to go on dates with are few and far between. Cathy has an awesome life . . . without a man. She lives in a great apartment, works hard, has a huge social network and is always saying yes to dinners and events and social engagements with interesting people in a variety of professions and of all ages. So it would be fitting, then, that she wouldn't just want *any* man to be able to be a part of her awesome world. It's not that she's extremely picky, she just knows what she wants, what she deserves and what she'll put up with. And what she'll put up with isn't a whole lot. Which, in turn, only makes the men chase her harder. Right now she's dating a super celebrity who is actually a really nice guy. And she's keeping *him* on his toes—not the other way around!

So how does she do it? Well, Cathy is the ultimate Catch.

From the Male Room

'There are many things that can get you to chase a woman. It could be the fact she has no baggage, that

she is really nice and that she comes across as very approachable. You chase a woman because she seems interesting. The type of woman that turns me on is a woman who is a bit sporty and she looks great when she is sweaty and likes to take pride in herself. Cooking is a must, and she must like animals and dancing.'—**Danny**

A Cautionary Tale: Camilla

'I'm a banker,' the smooth guy at the bar said to Camilla.

'Wow!' she replied, touching his bicep. It was hard and big.

'Yeah, girls usually cream themselves when I tell them I earn half a million.'

She didn't know how to take this so she gave a giggle, tossed a lock of expertly blow-dried hair out of her eyes and leaned in to listen more intently to him. The Banker told her that he worked at a big bank; that he was in mergers and acquisitions; and that he worked in the city. She knew the address. She was impressed. A banker. Just what I need, she thought, recalling her recent break-up from a dude who couldn't even hold down a job. And Mr Ex was skinny, no big biceps of his own. She'd never wanted a weedy boyfriend. And yet somehow she'd ended up with just that. She wondered how she'd dated him for so long.

'I never wanted to marry you,' Mr Ex had told her after they broke up. Never? She finally understood why he'd refused to commit after all those freaking years—he was a stringer; a man who liked to string a woman along for as long as he possibly could and, bam!, one day he lets her know that he never wanted to settle down with her and that marriage was never even on the cards. Jesus.

> ### #5. DON'T GET CAUGHT WITH A STRINGER
>
> A stringer is a man who constantly promises to commit to you, marry you, move in with you, but never actually takes action. Know it's not you, it's him.

Either way, at this particular moment Camilla didn't give a shit. She was a powerful single woman who was about to take on the world armed with a miniskirt and YSL stilettos (bought on sale!).

She looked at The Banker through her green eyes and gave a giggle at something he said. He passed her a third peach bellini. He was definitely cute, in a boyish kind of way. His sandy brown hair and big blue eyes were set off by his baby blue shirt. His tie sat loosely on his neck.

It was Friday night and Camilla and her best girl-friend, Kate—facialist to the stars (she was a genius with her fingers)—were at Rockpool restaurant in the hope of meeting hot bankers. And they had just landed themselves two of the hottest in the room.

Because here's how it works: bankers are hot property. Every girl in Sydney wants to bed one, date one, marry and make an honest man out of one. Good luck to those gals who are under the illusion that one of these men would actually make a good husband, considering in the banking world women are treated just like the stocks the bankers trade—commodities to be passed around and rated by their market value. Be too easy and your market value goes down. Be hard to get and your market value shoots so sky high that suddenly you're the most in-demand commodity on the public exchange list. And yet even at the top of the stockpile, you will still struggle mightily to find a banker who will treat you well—at least for longer than it takes to get you into bed.

But Camilla didn't care. She just wanted to feel desired again. Wanted. In demand. And The Banker was definitely able to do that for her. Yes, she looked at him again and surmised that he was definitely hot, hot property.

'Let's get out of here,' he whispered in her ear.

She cocked her head back and gave her signature glimmering smile. 'Where we going?' she purred back. God, I'm a little out of practice, *she thought. Although she wasn't doing too badly, especially considering she'd just come out of a long-term relationship and had only slept with three guys in her entire life, it was all coming back to her.*

After all, she had nailed Mr Ex—once the most eligible bachelor in all of the city before he started letting himself go. He was the impossible get and she had managed to nab him.

But he was old news. Lost his confidence, his mojo and his respect for himself when he'd lost his job in the financial crisis. And he hadn't bothered to do anything about it. Now she believed that drop kicks were out. Bankers were in.

She followed The Banker out of the restaurant. God, I'm tipsy, *she thought, giggling. She saw Kate out of the corner of her eye giving a wink. 'Go!' she mouthed to Camilla.*

And with that, he led her to a waiting cab, opened the door and, as soon as they got in, grabbed her neck and began to kiss her—amazing delectable kisses that tasted like strawberries—or maybe it was the aftereffects of the bellinis . . . But whatever, she was just happy to be in the arms of another man.

There was, Camilla Mason thought, something magical about the first few dates with a new man where the promise of sex was looming. Her skin was glowing, her hair was softer than ever and she could finally fit into the size 6 sass & bide leather pants she'd long been admiring. Not to mention the fact that The Banker was keeping up his end of the bargain too. He texted her the following day, and called her the next. Their conversations were electric. He made her laugh. He was smart, engaging and entertaining. Sure, she was rather desperate for any sort of connection—anything that would look good on paper (and even better lying next to her in her bed). Sure, she was fantasy jumping about a complete stranger—imagining all the wonderful things they could do together in their lives—but how bad could he be?

On the third day, his voice got urgent: 'I need to see you tonight.'

Really? Wow. And it was only Monday! Usually men waited a full week before they'd set another date, let alone the same week. He must like me, *she thought.* Brilliant.

In her new leather pants and off-the-shoulder white T-shirt studded with diamantes (she'd ditched her conservative knee-length skirts and wispy shirts the minute she'd become single again), she arrived at the pub

*he'd chosen for their meeting. Not exactly the first date
she'd envisioned.*

*He was already there, not exactly as good-looking as she'd
remembered him to be, wearing a leather jacket and jeans. In
fact, he was rather plain. And young. He couldn't be more than
26 years old.* God, had I been that drunk?

*'So . . .' he started, taking a big gulp of his drink. He
seemed nervous as he continued: 'The reason I asked you to
come tonight . . .'*

*She leaned in to listen intently. Was he married? Did he
have an STD? What the hell was so important?*

'I'm not really a banker . . .' He paused.

*Fuck. What? Um. Jesus. She didn't know where to look.
'OK . . .'*

*'Yep. I work at a pet store. My brother and I just say
we're bankers to pick up chicks.'*

Camilla was silent.

'So are you going to leave now?' he asked.

*'Um . . . no . . . definitely not,' she replied, darting her
gaze nervously around the room looking for an escape route.*

❤ #6.   TAKE TIME TO GET TO KNOW HIM

Get to know a man first before you start
making conclusions about your future
together. You never know what secrets he
may be hiding and it's best to have all the
information before you even contemplate
dating him for the long term.

What the fuck had just happened? Is this what's out there? Is this what the fuck I'm in for as a single girl? Men who lie about their jobs, take you to dingy pubs, lie about their age, and give you tests in order to get you into bed?

She drained her second drink and got out of there as fast as her heels could carry her. Honestly. What the!?

2

The Heartbroken Catch

Imagine this: you are sitting on your couch right now, and you know that you are ensconced in a great, fulfilling relationship with a man who not only ticks every single one of your ideal-man-list boxes, but who adds so much extra value into your life that you feel like you're on cloud nine every time you think about him. You know that when you see him you will be doted on, wooed, lavished with gifts, whisked away on romantic weekends, you'll hear from him when he says he will call, be cherished, fawned over, told you are beautiful all the time and you know you are generally supported by this person in your life who is not only totally hot and oozes sexuality, but actually thinks the same about you!

Because of this all-encompassing feeling of being wanted, cherished, loved and supported, it automatically emanates from every pore of your body every minute of the day—regardless of whether he is with you or not. Hence all the other men you come into contact with—whether it be at work, in the coffee shop, at the bar or on your daily walk—will instantly view you as the ultimate Catch. You are the woman these other men gawk at, look over and think, 'Wow, she's a Catch! I would love to have a girlfriend/wife/partner like that!'

It has nothing to do with the way you look or what you're wearing. Nor how big your boobs are or how short your skirt is, or how much money you have or where you work or what car you drive. Instead, it's all about the attitude that you project. You radiate a sexuality, confidence and natural awesomeness so strong that you'll be fantasised over by every man you come into contact with.

There are loads of these types of women walking around, and you know the type all too well. Men's heads turn and stare. They gape, and they line up to talk to her. Of course she won't have a bar of it, considering she's already ensconced in a wonderful relationship with the man of her dreams, but that doesn't matter. All the attention fuels her confidence and as she goes home to her man later that night, she knows she can get any man, but she has chosen him because of his great qualities. She appreciates him, and he appreciates her even more.

Now, stop the fantasy and get ready to start a new one. Imagine that you didn't have this man in your life.

#7. A TRUE CATCH ALWAYS ACTS THE PART

A true Catch doesn't have to have a man by her side to walk, talk, dress and act like a Catch. She is unattainable and the un-gettable get. She oozes confidence from every pore of her body and every man who comes into contact with her can sense this. She participates only in activities that empower her. She doesn't see herself as a desperate singleton and instead revels in her single life, loving her freedom and independence and milking every opportunity to enhance her life.

And that you were alone. And that it was just . . . you. You had no-one to back you up or tell you that you were beautiful or to fawn over and cherish you. All you had was yourself. It would be impossible to exude the same sort of charisma and sense of self, right? Wrong. That's where this book comes in. Becoming the ultimate Catch isn't about letting a man tell you that you are worthy or about him making you feel as though you've 'got it'. Instead, the exercises in this book are aimed at helping you find that inner strength, which will allow you to feel this good *all the time*, whether there's a man in your life or not. I know, I know—it sounds impossible, right? But it's not. Men no longer complete us. And that's not a bad thing either, considering we're in a different era now.

The era of the perpetually single girl

These days we're getting married later and later. There is more choice available to both men and women than ever before. Hence we are flitting from relationship to relationship, never quite wanting to settle down, or at least not being on the same page, relationship wise, as the other person. And with relationships being so transient and replaceable, we are being dumped and traded in for someone seemingly hotter, thinner, richer, *better*. We are being used, lied to, manipulated and then tossed aside like a piece of chewed gum. No wonder women's self-esteem has gone down the gurgler! No wonder we feel so incomplete! No wonder we have become a little desperate! And no wonder the men we are trying to court are sensing our state of unrest.

But when you morph from being The Toss to The Catch, and you begin to find your inner strength without a man, you will begin to attract a different calibre of man altogether. And he will want to hold on to you for dear life.

He will see you as his ultimate Catch, and having him in your life will be like the cherry on top of your already delicious cake. I realise that you might think that the last man you were with might have been the last man on the planet, or that you're sick to death of dating douchebag after douchebag, or that you can't seem to even get one date, no matter how hard you try or how many nights a week you go out. Do not fret. The Catch has none of these problems . . . and if you read on and practise all the exercises in this book, then you're about to become her: the ultimate Catch.

So you've just been dumped

While you might desperately want to become a Catch, you might also be stuck in what I like to call Planet I'm-in-love-with-my-ex. When you are so focused on trying to win back someone who clearly does not want to be with you, this hinders any chance you have of ever seeing what is right in front of you. Even if your soul mate hits you on the head with a sledgehammer, you won't notice them. They will be invisible to you. Or they might not dare approach you. As for the men who might be more suitable to you than the one who broke your heart? They won't view you as a Catch at all. Instead, there will be a gaggle of unsuitable men who will pursue you when you are broken. We'll discuss who those men are and how to spot them shortly. First, let's talk about why you might still be hung up on and hopeful about someone from your past.

The dude who broke your heart

Ah, the Big Fucking Break-up. Or as I like to call it, the BFB. You're at the lowest point you've been in a long, long time. Your self-esteem is down. Your life is no longer looking like it's going to turn out the way you'd hoped it would. And you're bummed about it. You think that if you could just talk to this person or let them see how great you are, and you could convince them to take you back, that everything would be better. Surprise—it won't.

Whether you've been in a long-term relationship, or whether you've been in something brief but which had you truly thinking they were 'the one', it's all the same. Heartbreak is heartbreak. And it sucks. It not only affects your mood and your emotions, but it can hurt physically too. Suddenly, eating, doing exercise or simply talking to friends and being around people becomes really, really painful. You believe that your last chance at happiness has been blown. You wonder how you can get him back. Or meet someone new. Or kill yourself. Whatever comes first.

Instead you are left lonely, desperate and unsure of what to do next. You constantly go over all the good memories, wishing that you could just have *one* more chance to show them how great you are and what a *huge* mistake they made by letting you go. And you constantly wonder what he is thinking and whether he, too, is thinking constantly of you.

As you sit there attempting to think about what went wrong, what the heck you did to lose him, and if perhaps there is something seriously wrong with you, you can almost feel a sharp pain inside your chest—it's as though your heart is literally shattering.

#8. CEASE ALL CONTACT

The process of getting over an ex is never a quick or simple one. They say time heals all, and it's true. But every contact you have with your ex will only set you back. It's like ripping off a band-aid again and again. Every time you do it, the sore will only take longer to heal. Leave the band-aid on and start creating an alternative life whereby your ex does not exist. Everyone goes through heartbreak so you're not the first. Not everyone understands (or remembers) the pain you are going through, but your sob stories will quickly get old if you attempt to regale anyone who will listen with your sorry tale. I wish there was a magic formula to getting over your ex. But the less you allow yourself to think about them or have contact with them, the faster your recovery time will be.

I know the feeling all too well. So do most of my friends. And ever since my BFB from an eight-year relationship, I've spent the past few years coming up with the only thing that ever works to get you over this heartache. Because until you do get over it, there is no point in even attempting to date again. You will not be perceived as The Catch, but rather as a singleton desperate to find the next man who will 'complete' you. Newsflash: it's not going to happen that way. Trust me—I learned the hard way.

So after you've had enough time on the couch, mooching around in front of the DVD player, checking your mobile phone every thirty seconds, praying he will call, something switches inside your head. Suddenly you want to find someone else. You want revenge. You want to feel good about yourself again. You rationalise that your boyfriend (when things were good) made you feel so great, safe, sexy and wanted! And you crave that feeling again. And you want it now. Surely the next man you meet will be able to fill in those blanks that are missing in your soul? At least that's what you're thinking. And so you head out searching for him— anywhere and everywhere—and believe you won't be happy until you find him.

But what becoming The Catch will teach you is that a man is not the answer to your happiness. If you believe that another man is the answer, you are going to be in deep, deep trouble and you will never reach Catch status. Because if you are not a full person

without a man, you are not going to attract a man
who is together, stable, secure and good enough for
the real you.

So here's the first exercise: can you remember a
time before you met the man who broke your heart?
Think back carefully. Think back to before you ever
had a boyfriend. You were single, and happy. You
probably spent a lot of time with your family and
friends. Perhaps you played a sport, went to the gym,
had more hobbies—did things you loved to do in
your spare time that made you feel fulfilled, happy and
in control. It doesn't matter what it was—the point is
you were so preoccupied, you didn't have hours upon
hours to sit and mull over the fact that there was no
guy in your life.

You never thought at that time that a man was
the answer to all your woes. Because here's another
newsflash: a man is *not* the answer. I repeat: a man is
not the answer to your happiness. He is the cherry on
the top of a multi-tiered cake which is bursting with
so many delicious fillings that if the cherry disappeared, there'd still be so much goodness deep inside
that you would still be fine. That's the point I need
you to get to. That's the essence of you becoming
The Catch. And you've been there before, so there
is no reason you can't get back there pretty fast. Just
follow the rest of the exercises in this book and I
guarantee you will be able to do this sooner than
you think.

Building yourself back up to being the full person who entered into your relationship in the first place is difficult, but it's imperative if you are ever going to be able to move forward—and eventually find someone new to be in a healthy, happy, long-term relationship with.

#9. BECOME WHOLE AGAIN ASAP

It's only natural to view yourself as half a person after your break-up. The other half of you has now vanished and you're left with a major gap in your life. Well, it's time to fill it back up again and build up the other half of yourself . . . on your own.

So let's hurry up and get started.

You put so much hope and effort into your past relationship. In your mind, you planned a future together. You wanted this to go well so badly that you pinned all your hopes and dreams on it. You imagined what life would be like together and you even made physical steps towards setting up that life. Suddenly it's blown up in your face. Was it you? Was it them? Was it the universe?

As all these negative thoughts start hurtling through your head like your brain is a pinball machine gone wrong, you are probably starting to believe that being with your ex was your last chance at real happiness. That he's the last man on the planet and that you are destined to die alone if you don't get him back immediately. Yes, you're clearly suffering from what most women who have just come out of a relationship suffer from: Planet I'm-in-love-with-my-ex.

You'll never be The Catch if you're not over him

Here's the rub: it doesn't matter how long you were together. Regardless of whether it was the first date, or whether you were ensconced in a ten-year relationship, you might still think that you are in love with this person. But when a man is in love with a woman, he will do anything—and I mean *anything*—to be with her and to make it work. Anything. He travels thousands of kilometres, makes sure he calls her when he says he will, takes note of important occasions in her life, and generally aims to please her *all the time*. I've seen it—men who are in love do indeed do this. And if your man isn't doing this for you any more, he has lost interest in you and there is *nothing* you can do about it, other than build yourself back up and transform into a Catch.

Because, in short, if a man is interested in you, he will do everything he can to see you and to have sex with you. And if he has stopped doing any of those things (or never started in the first place), he *doesn't want to be with you.*

#10. LET MEN CHASE YOU

The Catch only likes men who like her back. She doesn't chase unavailable men, players or bad boys. She doesn't run after lost causes or waste her precious time waiting for these types of men to pay her attention or ask her out or contact her when they said they would. If a man is not courting her in the proper ways, she doesn't beat herself up over it and then proceed to chase him. Instead, she simply knows that this isn't the man for her and swiftly moves on.

This might be a hard pill to swallow. And you might find yourself begging him for a reason as to why he has gone quiet. But here's the cold hard truth: when men decide that a relationship is over, it's over. They often don't know why they feel that way, or what exactly contributed to them no longer wanting to see you or have sex with you. Hence, no matter how many times you ask him, he might not even know the answer himself, so he's definitely not going to tell you what you want to hear any time soon.

Men and their emotions

If you're wondering what he's thinking or how he's coping living his life without you, stop right now. He's not even thinking of you. Or at least not right at this moment. He isn't reading a self-help book or mulling over romantic movies or talking for hours on end with his friends about why things went so horribly wrong. But it's not because he didn't care or because you're not good enough for him. It's just that most men aren't able to identify their feelings. And if any arise, they will simply quash them, drink beer, watch sport and go out with their mates. Men are not emotionally driven like women. Instead they find it difficult to identify their emotions and don't spend hours upon hours working out what went wrong in their minds or on the phone to their friends. And they most definitely won't communicate any of their real thoughts to you. At least not for a very long time—until way after you've given them ample space and time to come to terms with their emotions. The average time for men to be able to do this? It's around six months to one year before you'll even hear from him as to how he felt or still feels about you. Yes, that's the average time.

Which means that you now have at least *six months* of silence. Of hearing nothing that you want to hear from this man who has just broken your heart. You can live in hope that he will *eventually* come around and realise what he feels and decide to tell you. But the more you ask him, the more he is going to retreat and the less time he is going to spend on thinking of you or why he no longer wants to spend any time with you. In fact the more you mess with his timeline, the longer it's going to take him to eventually come around. That is just how the male biological break-up mind works. And there is absolutely *nothing* you can do about it.

#11. THE CATCH KNOWS NOT TO RUSH MEN

Unfortunately men do not process thoughts and feelings as fast as women do. Instead they ignore them, drink beer and go out with their mates. You are not on their mind or, if you are, they certainly won't be telling *you* about it. Which means you have to move on with your life without him. No calls, no texts, no emails, no pining over him. Moving on means building yourself up into the ultimate Catch. And only once you do that, will he — or any man for that matter — start to chase you.

Rocking up to his pad in your sexiest lingerie or crying on the phone to him, incessantly texting him, begging him for an explanation—all this is simply going to delay the process he needs in order to finally realise what he has lost and then tell you why he royally messed up.

So stop right now. Put down your phone. Close your laptop. Stop stalking him on Facebook. Delete his number. And pretend he no longer exists. Easier said than done, so here's how to do it.

Exercise

To expedite this process, take a blank piece of paper and divide it into two columns.

On the left-hand side, write down all the things that you disliked about the guy you were dating. Make them as superficial, deep, detailed and numerous as possible. Go nuts. Go on.

On the other side of the page, write the opposite of each quality. These are the things you *do want* in a partner. Make sure they are positive statements. For example, if your ex was anti-social, don't write 'someone who is not anti-social'. Instead, write something like, 'very social, warm and friendly to everyone'.

If your ex was untrustworthy, didn't listen to your problems, was unsupportive of your goals, unaffectionate, unreliable or inconsistent, make sure that you list on the opposite side all the corresponding *good* qualities. Make the demands on the right side of your page as outrageous and dream-like as possible. And make sure they are all positive statements that are written in the present tense. We are going to train your subconscious to focus on these amazing qualities so that not only do you instantly see them when someone new comes along and chases you, but you instantly realise that you shouldn't be with someone who has the opposite of these qualities.

Now, I want you to take a photo of this list with your phone. I want you to read the positive side of the list every night before you go to bed and repeat the most important qualities to yourself whenever you can—whether you are in the shower, on the train, on a walk, whatever. And every time you think of the person you are no longer with in an unhealthy, longing way, I want you to read the negative side of the list and then repeat the positive qualities to yourself in the present tense.

Personally, all the guys I'd been dating at one stage of my single life seemed to share one common trait: they would lie. And so, on my positive side, I wrote down the word 'trustworthy'. Every time I was on a walk or in the shower or had a spare moment to think about the type of man I wanted to be with, I would repeat the word 'trustworthy' to myself. I would shut my eyes and bathe in the warmth of the knowledge that I was with someone trustworthy—even though I was single.

This process of *feeling* as though you are already with someone who has all the qualities that you have on your list, even though you haven't met him yet, is an extremely powerful process. It is so powerful, in fact, that if you can connect with it as often as possible and truly believe that you have found someone with those qualities then you will meet them. I guarantee you. If you haven't learned about the power of the universe yet, now is the time to do it.

When you are vacillating between being unsure about your ex and feeling so low you are begging for him back while attempting (hoping) to find someone

---

♥ #12. MR UNAVAILABLES PREY ON WEAK WOMEN

The newly single girl is never going to be seen as a Catch by her ultimate man. She will attract men who prey on weak women—and they will always be unavailable, whether they're commitment-phobes or are already in a relationship or simply are just after some 'fun'. He might pretend to be the perfect, doting man when you meet him in the bar, the club or at the supermarket, but pretty soon after you start sleeping with him, his true colours will shine through. And then you will lose all hope in men. As much as it's imperative to watch out for these types, it's even more important to avoid dating to find 'the one' when you're still in a vulnerable position. Read on to find out how to flip yourself—and, in turn, the guys you attract—around.

---

new, you will run into big trouble. Because instead of finding men who are real, true potentials, you only date Mr Unavailables. I should know. When my eight-year relationship first ended, I dated three men in a row who, unbeknown to me, actually had girlfriends. That's right—*three*. At the time I had no idea why it was happening to me. Hence I blamed the men, my judgement, the state of modern dating—anything but the fact that I was actually not ready to get back out there, and therefore was only able to attract men who weren't ready or available for something serious with me either.

#13. KNOW THAT MEN DO *NOT* COMPLETE YOU

You complete yourself. And the sooner you realise that, the better off you'll be. You have a fabulous life and you are extremely cautious about who you will let in to share that wonderful life with you.

The problem with getting back into the game too soon

Coming out on the other side of it all with your dignity, self-respect and standards intact is easier said than done. I know all too well about the fact that your boyfriend was your other half. And that you are now alone. And you feel incomplete. There is nothing to give you confidence, raise your self-esteem or even to get you out of bed in the morning.

'Will anyone ever love me as much?' you ponder. Hence you become desperate to find something—anything—to replace what you had. You are missing a piece of yourself and find going on without replacing that missing piece with someone else—preferably someone who is shinier, newer, sexier and more compatible with you—incomprehensible. Unfortunately there is absolutely no rushing this process. Especially considering the fact that the symptoms you experience as a result of the BFB make you all the more a target for the Mr Unavailables.

The symptoms of being the Heartbroken Catch

- You are desperate to meet a man.
- You start giving men you see out and about the Desperate Eyes (DEs).
- You drive yourself nuts looking for men.
- You pounce on any man who gives you attention.
- You think every man you meet is potentially 'the one'.
- You attract men who like to prey on weak women.
- You sleep with men too soon because you are so desperate for some physical closeness with someone—anyone—who you think will make you feel whole again.
- You do crazy things.
- You are up and down emotionally.
- Men will constantly disappoint you because the ones you are attracting are not worthy of you.

The solution

You need mourning time. I'm sorry to say it, but jumping right back onto the dating bandwagon—unless you are Superwoman—means you're going to draw in those guys who are only in it for one thing. Bonus—they're masters at hiding their intentions too. So what's going to happen is you're going to waste a hell of a lot of time and energy with these sorts, and then you're going to end up even more lonely, depressed and desperate. You're going to become one of those women who start to ask where the heck are all the good guys, and then you're going to become a sad singleton.

I remember one night after my break-up, I was out with my girlfriends for dinner at a local steakhouse. I spotted a table of a group of around twenty men. At the end of the table sat the hottest guy I'd ever seen. I'd been single for two weeks. I stared at him like he was the last spoon of dessert, while my girlfriends continued to chat away about things more interesting (and important) than who my next boyfriend was going to be.

Eventually, one of the men at the table noticed me staring and came over to say hi.

'What's her story?' he asked my girlfriend, pointing to me.

'Oh her?' my girlfriend replied. 'She's newly broken-up from an eight-year relationship. She's a little desperate right now.'

'Oh yeah, I can tell. We can all tell.'

Yikes. Not that I really cared. All I was focused on was getting to meet the hot guy at the end.

'So . . . who's your hot friend?' I asked the guy, pointing at my new crush. 'He's cute. Is he single?'

'Listen here,' he said, looking me squarely in the eyes. 'You are doing the worst possible thing a single girl can do: you are giving him the Desperate Eyes.'

My girlfriends burst out laughing, but I didn't find it at all amusing.

'How am I supposed to indicate to a man that I'm interested if I don't try and catch his eye?' I asked, confused.

'Not doing what you're doing.'

Instead, he proceeded to give me a task: to sit at home for the next five days . . . on my own, with no dates, no men and no distractions.

'You need to become a person again without relying on a man to make you happy. You need to learn how to do that before you even think of being able to attract another man.'

I didn't exactly know what he was talking about. But over the next year, I figured it out. It wasn't easy, let me tell you. I experienced a year of every type of dating faux pas, every caddish man, every bad date, every feeling of pain, loneliness and aloneness.

Until one day I got burned so badly, I realised that things had to change, pronto. And so I invented a way to inject power back into myself. Learn from my own

#14. SMILE BUT NEVER STARE

In order to catch the attention of a man you think is cute, make a quick glance at him across the room. Catch his eye, smile and then look away. Do not look back at him again. Chances are if you held his gaze for around three seconds, he will have noticed. If he wants to talk to you, he will come over and he'll feel as though he's the one making the effort. If, however, you continue to stare at him for the remainder of the evening, he won't think it's sexy, he'll think it's creepy. The Desperate Eyes never work at anything other than scaring men away.

mistakes. And the funniest part of it all was that after I completed my 30-Day Catch Boot Camp (which you'll be introduced to in Chapter 7), the same man I had spotted at the end of the table who wouldn't even look in my direction found me on Facebook and—you guessed it—he asked me out!

Post-break-up checklist for the Heartbroken Catch

1. Book an appointment with a therapist.
2. Delete all your old emails from your ex. If you can't bear to part with them, send them to a friend

or copy and paste them into a password-protected document on your desktop.

3. Get a hobby—seriously. Start boxing/dancing/ writing—whatever your heart desires. You're about to have a whole lot of spare time.

4. Go nuts in the bookshop's self-help aisle. Read everything you can about breaking up, moving on, finding true love, baking a cake to get back your man—anything. And then once you've read all you can, stay the heck away from any of those books.

5. Go easy on his Facebook. And then when you can muster up the strength to do it, delete him. There's no need to stalk him. It only causes more pain and you don't need that right now.

6. Wait for him to change his relationship status on Facebook. Only then should you change yours. And even then, I advise not making it too public by deleting 'no longer in a relationship' from your public feed. And definitely do not put up on your Facebook profile that you're now 'single'. It looks desperate and cheap. You're The Catch. You're not single and looking for anyone who doesn't desperately want to catch *you*.

7. Only have positive things to say about your ex. Be the stronger one. Even if they cheated—zip it.

8. Only go on a date when you're ready. It's perfectly fine to deflect dates by admitting you've just come

out of a long-term relationship and you're happy being single for a while.

9. Find four activities that make you deliriously happy, and that you can do at any time with little cost. Mine were jogging on the beach; eating a chicken wrap from a specific store (seriously); looking at furniture stores; and drinking dandelion tea with my best friend.

10. Use your money that you would have spent on the two of you on yourself, wisely. Instead of throwing it away on booze, take it and book in a weekly blow-dry, mani/pedi, personal training sessions (you can get boxing classes from $10!), go for walks, and use this time and energy to focus on yourself. Instead of having to make dinner for two every night at 6 pm, I turned that into my running time. Getting fit was definitely one of the joys that emerged from my break-up.

11. Go as *nuts* as you want. And don't listen to anyone who is telling you that you are manic. It will pass. You are grieving. You are mourning. You are going through a time in your life where you are half the person you were when you were with your partner. You are not yet The Catch. And therefore you are not yet ready to find The Catch and to allow him into your life. Don't fret. It's not your time yet, but it will come.

12. Be careful of casual sex and be safe at all times.

A Cautionary Tale: Meg

Meg Johnson woke up, head pounding, in a strange bed, with an even stranger man snoring beside her. Ouch! *she thought, holding her hand to her head, the taste of tequila still in her throat. Her gaze darted around the room, searching in the darkness for her underwear (only La Perla for Meg) and the skimpy black lace dress she had worn the night before. She carefully pulled back the thick cream bed sheet (so sumptuous, she noticed) and tiptoed to the other side of the bed.* Fuck! *she winced, stubbing her toe on the corner of a chest of drawers. She glanced over at the man in the bed and breathed a sigh of relief when he didn't stir. Meg had no patience for niceties in the mornings. This was a one-night, and nothing more. She didn't want a phone call the next day.*

She thought back to how she'd ended up there—butt-naked, at 8 am on a Sunday morning. She'd attended her best friend Camilla's birthday party at a hot club in the city the night before and she'd spotted Camilla talking to a tall, dark-haired man. When Meg sauntered over to see who this handsome creature was, Camilla instantly palmed him off onto Meg.

'Meg, meet John—we work together! You two will have a blast!'

Meg's eyes had instantly lit up.

'I'm Meg. A Sagittarius,' she said, extending a well-manicured hand.

'John. Not into star signs.' He smiled. Meg melted. Suddenly an insatiable urge flooded through her body. She

wanted John instantly inside of her, and began wondering how he'd feel about doing it with her in the bathroom. After all, she wasn't wearing her bright red La Perlas for nothing.

She put her best flirtatious moves onto him: jutting out breasts; nodding in all the right places; asking all the right questions; and surreptitiously slipping in key sexual buzzwords like 'G-string', 'La Perla' and 'threesome' into her sentences. Within twenty minutes, her mission was accomplished: he was inviting her to have a drink back at his place. What followed from there was the usual Meg Johnson Show—drinking, stripping, acrobatic sexual moves, tantalising sexual favours and her feigning sleep and then slipping out without so much as a kiss goodbye or the swapping of phone numbers.

While they usually say that men want sex and women want love, Meg Johnson was the exception to the rule. She wanted sex, and would do anything to get it. She was one of those single women who emanated a need and desire for sex so strong that men flocked to her in droves to get a taste of it. There was something about the feeling of being vulnerable and naked in front of a strange man that turned her on, made her feel powerful, invincible—she could achieve anything. She never got emotionally attached to any of these men (or at least hardly ever), and never seemed to have a shortage of hot bodies ripe for the picking.

She wasn't the prettiest of her friends, but she was damn good at the art of seduction. And her sleek, blonde-highlighted bob, high cheekbones and impeccable figure—she'd made sure that her daily running schedule and gruelling workouts meant her body was immaculate, not to mention the fact she'd had a boob job the minute she turned 18—was a winning combination that never failed to impress the men she targeted.

But the years had passed, and Meg wasn't 18 any more. In fact, the last few months Meg found she wasn't having as much fun as she once did. All this sex . . . all this no-strings intimacy . . . all these conversations with all these different men—something finally snapped inside of Meg that morning. As she stepped out of John's apartment in her crinkled outfit, the blinding sunlight hit her like a sledgehammer. This was the fourth time she had woken up in a strange bed with a strange man this month, and suddenly she had a revelation: she wanted out.

She grabbed her mobile phone and dialled Camilla.

'Meg? Are you okay?' Camilla answered sleepily.

'Yeah, just need to talk—can you meet me for breakfast?'

'Sure, where are you?'

'I have no fucking idea.'

When Camilla arrived at the girls' favourite café at Bondi Beach, she found a pale-looking Meg still in the same outfit as the night before, wearing dark glasses (Meg always kept them in her handbag for moments like these) and gulping from an extra-strong-looking long black. Meg knew Camilla wasn't even surprised to see her best friend looking this way. In fact, this sort of behaviour was beginning to become eerily familiar.

**#15. CASUAL SEX IS GREAT . . .
UNTIL IT'S NOT**

The Catch doesn't get herself a reputation
for sleeping around. She might do it in secret
overseas or on a cruise ship, but when she's
in her own environment she ensures that her
reputation stays pristine. Sex is fun but when
you're ready to meet 'the one' you want to
make sure that you haven't slept with his
best friend, brother, cousin or flatmate. Be
very discerning about who you sleep with
early on so that you don't ruin your chances
when the right one comes along.

---

*Meg looked up at Camilla and, even through her dark
glasses, Camilla noticed her eyes looked a little vacant.*

*'I can't remember what I've said to which person or where
I'm up to in my stories or what I'm supposed to be like with
each person,' Meg said absentmindedly as she continued to
gulp her coffee. 'I mean seriously—how am I going to know
when it's real if with every person I have to pretend like
it's real?'*

*Camilla's head jerked up in surprise, especially
considering that in the past month, Meg had been involved
in flings with an ex, a famous TV star she'd met at a bar,
and even had a threesome. Oh, and Camilla had no doubt
that Meg had fucked John too.*

'It's never affected me like this,' Meg said. 'But perhaps a combination of the summer heat, the hangovers and the various sizes and shapes of dicks—'

'And one vagina, don't forget!' Camilla interjected, referencing the threesome Meg had found herself in one summer afternoon.

'Yeah, that . . . well, it's all led me to this point. It might be enough . . .' Her voice trailed off softly.

'Well, you can always just stop,' Camilla snapped, staring Meg intently in the eye.

'No, I can't. Because I'm a sex item.' Meg glanced down at her cleavage, a small smile springing to her lips. It was as though her body gave her immense pleasure and she wasn't content unless some strange man was sharing in the joy too.

Meg picked up the salt shaker from the breakfast table and began examining it like it was a part of the male anatomy. Not that sex was the only thing on Meg's mind. Oh no. She was smart. And good at her job. She had been a high-flying government advisor. That was how the two girls had met— Camilla the reporter and Meg setting up the interviews with the various politicians. She'd moved quickly up the ladder— until she started fucking the boss.

Meg remembered the day well. He'd called her into his office and closed the door behind him.

'I'd like to nurture you,' he told her. 'I can see you're a bright young talent. A group of us are going to London for a political conference. Want to join?'

She had been flattered beyond belief, and had packed up her best London winter chic outfits. She'd found it odd that *she'd gotten to travel business class, while the rest of the team travelled economy.*

'A mix-up with the seating arrangement,' her boss had said. But when he invited her up to his room that night after they'd all shared dinner, she knew it wasn't exactly a mistake that she'd been invited to sit next to him the entire flight.

The sex—as she thought of it—was 'old'. 'It was like having sex with my dad,' she'd whispered on the phone to Camilla the following morning.

'You'd better watch it, Meg,' Camilla replied, clicking her tongue. 'He's got a wife, two kids under ten—and your job could be on the line if anyone found out.'

'Oh, they won't,' she said in a whisper. 'He's very discreet.'

Discreet they were. For six bloody months she fucked and blew him at every opportunity they got to be alone together. There were hotel rooms, late nights in his office, overseas trips and weekends away. It was all very glamorous for Meg at the time. That was until . . .

#16. THE CATCH DOESN'T HAVE AFFAIRS

It's not fair on the other woman and it's mightily degrading. Women with low self-esteem fall for the crap that is dished out by taken men. Catches do not. Catches see themselves having a real, honest future. And if he's cheated on his partner, he's going to cheat on you too.

'Hello? Are you listening to me? I said you need to take a hiatus . . .' Camilla was saying. 'No more sex for a little while. Can you try to do that?'

Meg was silent. She wasn't quite sure whether Camilla was just being judgemental, or whether she really did indeed have a point.

'Listen to me,' Camilla continued. 'You're starting to get a name. People are talking. You've got to stop having sex with every Tom, Dick or Harry who looks at your crotch and tells you that you have nice tits. You do, OK?'

At that moment, Meg spotted the cute waiter giving her the eye. Hmmm, I'd love a piece of that, she thought, eyeing his biceps and the bulge in his pants. Maybe one last sexual sojourn couldn't be so bad . . .

 #17. **DON'T BE AFRAID TO TAKE A DATING HIATUS**

When you start to feel that your dating schedule or your sex life is taking over your life and depleting you of energy, don't be afraid to put a hold on it all. Simply stop, take a step back and go on a hiatus. You have every right to say no to dates, no to sex and no to seeing someone who you don't feel like seeing any more for as long as you'd like. Take this time to focus on getting your strength and power back up and you'll be better for it in the long run. Don't be afraid of missing out either—if a man likes you enough, he'll wait for you!

3

Moving on without shooting yourself in the foot

#18. **STOP GIVING MEN THE DESPERATE EYES (DEs)**

These are the eyes a lot of single women give to any eligible man they spot. The trouble is that these eyes scare a man away faster than a game. Desperate Eyes let every man you meet know you're not The Catch.

Of course the men who spot women giving the DEs will respond with wide eyes and a bulge in their pants. After all, no man is going to say no to the advances of a pretty girl. The trouble is that when you're fresh off the boat from a break-up, expectations are muddled. She's thinking as soon as she meets him, 'He's "the one"!' He's thinking, 'She's the one for tonight!' In fact here's how it really works. When a man meets a woman for the first time, the very first thought in his head is this: 'Would I fuck her?' His very next thought is:

'And if I would fuck her, how much is it going to cost me?'

That is it. That is all he's thinking. The more it costs him—in terms of his time, his effort, his energy, his chivalry—and the harder he has to work to get you, the more he begins to value you as The Catch.

Women, on the other hand, respond entirely differently. It's not our fault either: it's our biology that does it to us. Our biology makes us look at men as potential partners, not bonk buddies. And since we get one egg per month, our bodies tell our minds to be very discerning about who we have sex with. Sure, there are many women out there who attempt to defy this source of female instinctual behaviour. So they hop from man to man, having sex whenever they want to, in secret hope of finding 'the one' without getting scathed, battered, bruised and heartbroken along the way. But guess what ends up happening? The more they date, sleep with random men and try to find 'the one', the more they lose their sense of self, their identity and their power. And then they attract the wrong sorts of men, over and over again. And then they start to doubt themselves, and their worth. And then they wonder where all the good men are!

Here's a newsflash for you: there are good men everywhere. That's right—I said it. *Everywhere.* It's just that you won't be able to see them clearly—or rather, they won't be able to see you—because you will be giving off desperate, needy vibes that will not only attract the wrong sorts of men, but will, in turn, make you a woman who men will want to toss, not catch.

So how do you morph from The Toss into The Catch that every man wants to fight for and pin down? Well, it takes time. There is no short cut to it either.

I won't lie to you: morphing yourself from being tossed to being caught is damn hard work. Some women have it naturally, but many women have to work at it bloody damn hard. Including me.

After Jackie ended a relationship with her boyfriend of five years, suddenly she was no longer the taken girl, she was The Anti-Catch. Or at least that's what her inner subconscious was yelling out. She was 34 and thought she'd be married by then, with a kid in tow. Therefore her negative energy about herself meant that she was not attracting men who wanted to spend the rest of their lives with her, but rather men who only saw her as Miss Fun. Certainly, at the time, she thought they were wonderful men and each time she pinned all her hopes and dreams on them. But after one or two months, when they began to sense that she was after something more than just 'fun', she was tossed right back into the treacherous dating ocean without so much as a text message goodbye.

'But I thought I had so much to offer! I'm smart! I'm not overweight, don't have a criminal record and can even make a mean chocolate brownie! So what the heck is going on?' she asked me at the time.

#19. BE UNATTAINABLE AND HE'LL CHASE YOU MORE

If you find yourself in a merry-go-round of dating men who only think of you as 'Miss Fun' and nothing more, then heed a word of warning: you are giving in to them too easily. They are getting exactly what they desire too quickly, easily and cheaply. Sure, they will tell you all the right things up front, but the fact that you're making it so easy for them makes them think that you're just up for fun. Being unattainable means that the men who are only after fun will get bored with having to chase you and you'll be better able to weed out these types. This means not kissing, having sex or even going back to a man's house until he has proven his worth and seriousness to you. It's okay to tell a man that you don't 'do' any of those things unless you're serious about someone. Don't be afraid to lose him — he should feel lucky to even be able to hang out with you in the first place.

Looking back, she can see it clearly now: she was being *that* girl—the one who men simply don't want to make their girlfriend. The same thing happened to me too. But it took me almost one whole year to figure out a foolproof methodology to turning myself

#20. SMART GIRLS CAN BECOME DUMB WHEN THEY'RE SEARCHING FOR LOVE

Even the smartest woman can be stupid when it comes to dating. Because The Catch isn't the smartest girl in the room or the prettiest. She is the one who knows her worth and isn't afraid to deny anything that might be less.

from The Toss to The Catch. Finally, after one whole year of dating, mating and major self-introspection, the calibre of men I started to attract began to change, but only when I finally started to believe (and know in my heart) that I could get the one that I wanted. And that the one would actually want me back. And that when I did finally meet him, there would no games, no mixed messages, no delayed text messages or cancelled dates—none of it. And guess what? It worked. As it did for Jackie too.

No more players. No more Mr Funs. No more Mr Unavailables. No more requests for one-night stands. Those days were over. But I'll say it again: there is no getting around this journey, this process. It will take as long as it needs to take and, until you are ready, the more you desperately look for him without first becoming The Catch, the harder he'll be to find.

It's so interesting to me to look back on my journey and see how my personality and the way I viewed myself

---

#21. GAMES WILL BE A THING OF THE PAST WHEN YOU MEET THE RIGHT PERSON

The reason you might feel like every man plays games, or is a player, is because you're constantly ending up with the wrong sorts of men. When the right one rolls around, there will be no games, no delayed text messages, no mixed signals. Things will be easy, seamless, enjoyable and stress free.

---

was actually a catalyst for what type of men I was drawing in. I was weak, vulnerable and desperate. And therefore I was attracting the type of men who preyed on weak women. The *worst* type of men. I knew I had to build up my strength. But I didn't know how. And so I created the 30-Day Catch Boot Camp (see p. 137).

After I completed the program, I had friends begging to know my secret: 'How do you do it? How did you change yourself so dramatically? You look the same! So what's changed?'

My mindset, that's what changed. I helped Jackie through this process, and hundreds of women after her. And now it's your turn. Your life can change too. While I put in an enormous amount of effort and personal work into my mental and physical state, the fact is anyone can do it, if you want it badly enough. So I want you to say goodbye to being the girl who gets tossed aside, and welcome in the girl who is viewed as

The Catch by every man she comes across. And if you follow the 30-Day Catch Boot Camp plan, I guarantee you, it won't be long before you will be caught by the ideal man. So grab yourself a glass of wine (or a shot of tequila!) and let's get cracking.

#22. STRONG WOMEN WIN THE GAME

It might be tough to fathom now, but you need to build up your strength if ever you want to attract a strong man. Take the time to do it right—there is no need to rush this process. Start now and don't ever look back.

Men tell me all the time there's a major difference between The Catch and The Toss. While it's often tough for them to articulate exactly what she looks like, they always express the same sentiment. There are many subcategories of The Toss and it's imperative that you understand who these women are and their characteristics and behavioural traits in order to avoid becoming her, or at least knowing that the reason you are not able to find love any time soon is because you were once her.

The SADFAB

The SADFAB—Single and Desperate For a Boyfriend—is needy, distressed, urgently wants a boyfriend or a husband, and is always on the lookout for one. She wants to impress men, and constantly thinks of ways to do it. She thinks she's supposed to *do* things for men in order to get them to like her more. She gives them sexual favours, buys them presents, calls them, texts them, waits for their calls, offers to pay for their dinner, and is always trying to make plans, make decisions for them and corner them into committing to her.

'So where is this going?' she'll ask by the second date. She thinks all this will work because she doesn't understand how the male mind works. She also sees husband hunting as a type of sport that women should engage in.

The Husband Hunter

While the SADFAB and the Husband Hunter (HH) are not mutually exclusive, let me explain why, if you are anything remotely reminiscent of a Husband Hunter, you should stop right now. Here is the tale of Courtney, a typical HH.

When Courtney's four-month fling ended, she simply wanted to go straight from the pick-up to the next relationship. I laughed and told her it doesn't work like that—there's a process. Everyone needs to take time to work out what went wrong in their past relationship and fix up patterns in their own behaviour before jumping into the next.

Men seem to know all about this process—almost intuitively. And they don't ever try to rush it. They simply have fun and revel in the opportunity to meet new people and learn more about the opposite sex through talking, casual dating and the simple art of getting to know someone. Sure, most of the time they're trying to get into your pants too, but if you delay it for just a little while, you'll notice that many men are curious as to what women want, how to please women and how to be good boyfriend material. Hence the astute ones will ask questions and try to figure you out a little bit more. They won't jump headfirst into asking you about your five-year plan or ascertain whether or not you'll commit to them and immediately become exclusive. Oh no. They don't have a ticking biological clock—and their lack of agenda actually makes you want to hang around them more!

From the Male Room

'Too many women just want to get married and have kids right away. You go on a date with them and it's extremely awkward. I want a girl with her own career ambitions and someone who is actually doing something with her life. Ask any guy and these days a career is so important. If her sole goal is to find a husband, she's definitely not even going to get a boyfriend.'—**Gabe**

The trouble with women is that many are way too focused on the endgame. When I asked a bunch of men what was the number-one thing they hated about dating, they told me it was the fact that all women are way too quick to judge them on their ability to commit; the endgame is always on women's minds. But for the men, the destination is far from their thoughts.

Case in point is the story told to me by my friend Doug as I accompanied him to one of his work functions. He pointed out the husband-hunting women in the room. You could see by their outfits, their body language and the way their eyes darted around the room in desperate search for 'him' that they weren't just out to have a good time.

#23. DRESS CLASSILY

When you are attending an event where you know there is going to be a load of husband-hunting women in a room filled with eligible men, try dressing classily rather than sexily. A pair of killer heels, well-fitting jeans and a crisp shirt with your hair tied back will stand out to the good guys more so than the woman in the see-through top and skirt so short that you can see her knickers. Quality men will be drawn to quality-looking women. The players will go for the obvious score. Work out what you want and dress accordingly.

'I see these women everywhere I go,' he told me.
'They follow eligible men around the room with Desperate Eyes and it's blatantly obvious that they're sizing
him up for potential husband material even before he's
opened his mouth. Men are never going to respond
well to that. Why can't women understand that there's
a process, and that process starts with a simple, friendly
conversation with *no* agenda?'

He explained to me that in order to truly find a
husband, the hunting needs to stop and women need to
start living fulfilled lives without a bloke by their side
before one will become even remotely interested.

'What's so good about marriage anyway?' he asks
me. 'So many marrieds are so miserable. I'd rather be
single.' Perhaps he has a point. Even if you desperately
do want a husband, you need to *act* (at least for the part
of meeting men) like you don't.

The Sex Item

The Sex Item is extremely problematic because she ruins
the dating game for the rest of us. Why should a man
wait to have sex with you, when he can have it instantly
with The Sex Item? But on the flip side, she can do some
of us a bit of a service, because eventually (pretty quickly
actually), men get rather bored of constantly having to
do it with Sex Items. The sex they're getting becomes
unfulfilling, even a little boring. And that's exactly the
point at which they decide to go and look for The

Catch—the antithesis of The Sex Item. The minute
The Catch mentions that she's not one to rush sex and
that it's much nicer to be intimate with someone who
you respect and have gotten to know, that's when something will click inside the mature man's mind, and his
commitment gene will snap into shape.

#24. QUIT HAVING SEX TOO SOON

While you might want to be perceived by
men as a 'modern woman' who can do it
'like a man', in reality these modern women
are not winning. Having sex too soon almost
always, *always* ends badly. Just going back
to a man's place prematurely sends across
the wrong signals, even though he tells you
he wants you to and that it won't change
the way he feels about you. It will. Stay out
of the bedroom until you get to know him
without getting physical.

From the Male Room

'I would expect a woman to suggest that she is inter-
ested in having a boyfriend. What else would she
be interested in? Casual sex? As if! Free meals? A
chauffeur service? It is certainly not "desperate" for a
woman to be seeking a boyfriend.'—**Shane**

'There is no right time to have sex. I will say this though: I have never ever once had the experience where I dated a woman more than five times and then slept with her after that. It seems after five dates, if we haven't slept together, she's probably not interested. So now I assume that, if it hasn't happened by the fifth date, or at least there is a clear timeline and pathway to it happening, I am in the "friend zone" and it is never going to happen. That said, I am a very patient guy and would not be against going on ten dates with a girl before I will give up.'—**Steve**

The Bitch

You can be as bitchy as you want to men in the hope that they'll fall in love with you. But let me assure you that the type of man you want to attract is not going to find The Bitch even remotely attractive. Instead, he's going to get pretty bored of all her drama really quickly. He's not going to want a bar of her past the first few dates and he's going to toss her aside for a nicer girl. Being a nice girl doesn't mean you have to be all gushy and gooey with your man either. It just simply means not being a bitch.

You might be the smartest girl you know. You might have a great job, be CEO of a company and the fittest girl at the gym. But you might not be a Catch. Instead, you might encompass one or more of these off-putting qualities. Don't be too hard on yourself. No-one ever stopped to tell you that it might be your misguided behaviour that is scaring the men away. Just be aware of it and when you find yourself falling into any of these patterns, pull back, stop and ask yourself, 'What would a Catch do?'

From the Male Room

'I've got one girl currently sexting me. Am I interested in her? Not as much as the girl I have to chase. Then there's this other girl I'm mad about. She's not as easy to get. I'm chasing her. I feel like I can't quite have her yet and I know I'm going to have to try mightily hard to get her. The girl who is sexting me is just temporary. But she doesn't know that.'—**Jed**

A Cautionary Tale: Kate

It was the night after Camilla's birthday party and Kate Bloom was feeling particularly vulnerable.

'What the fuck happened last night?' she wondered, looking at the bruise on her arm. The bump on her head was beginning to throb and she had the taste of iron in her mouth. She vaguely remembered what had transpired: sculling shots of Grey Goose with her new boyfriend Zip before the party; Zip asking her if she'd move in with him (after one month!?); Zip getting violent; Zip throwing her against the wall; Kate running out of the house; Kate hearing the glass smash against the door behind her; Kate holding back her tears; Kate putting on a brave face at the party, but in reality wondering how her life had become so fucked up. She was 35 years old: no boyfriend, no assets, no life.

As she surveyed the scene in her apartment (thank god he'd left after the fight), all the bad memories of what it was like to grow up in a household where peace and quiet were faraway notions, and mornings of cracked glasses and chaos, came flooding back. She pushed them out of her mind and decided that she needed to get out and go for a run—immediately. It was the only thing that cleared her head, made her feel strong and in control of her life.

As Kate slipped on her crop top and tore a brush through her glossy, mahogany hair, she marvelled at her appearance in the mirror. She was, after all, one of those exceptionally gorgeous, smart, sophisticated and cool women who could get any man they desired. And yet she had one specific problem when it came to men: she was not into normal men. With normal jobs. Or normal lifestyles. The men she was interested in were otherwise known in psychiatrist's circles as Bad Boys.

#25. WOMEN ADDICTED TO BAD BOYS NEED TO BREAK THE PATTERN . . . PRONTO!

A Bad Boy addiction is symptomatic of low self-esteem and being stuck in a rut and so any excitement will do. To get rid of this addiction, it takes serious work and reprioritising of what you want. You need to see these men for what they are and realise they will never give you the future you deserve.

Kate Bloom was a woman addicted to this subset of the male species. Something about being around a man who wielded a gun in his spare time made her all the more drawn to him. Perhaps it was the fact that she was an instinctual 'rescuer'; perhaps it was her own crazy childhood with an abusive father that made her feel more comfortable around those sorts of men; perhaps it was the fact that her first love was the baddest of bad boys and she became addicted to the lifestyle and the euphoric feeling the relationship ignited in her heart. Either way, this was her pattern and it was only getting worse.

Not that her only interest was boys. In fact, it was quite the opposite for Kate. While she certainly attracted the worst of them (at the best of times), she was a career woman at heart. After graduating magna cum laude from one of the top business schools in the country, she'd changed course after a car accident forced her to quit her high-flying banking job for a prolonged stint in hospital. After her shocking death scare, she decided to go into something she was more passionate about. Hence she worked her way up in the beauty industry to become the uber facialist of choice to the stars. Vogue *magazine had recently featured her as one of its top ten bright young beauticians to watch out for, and since then, the phone had been ringing off the hook. She was booked up for months and had become the go-to girl who was responsible for giving that coveted Hollywood glow to the world's hottest women (and many of the men!).*

But when she wasn't working, she couldn't help attracting the bad boys.

The latest was Zip, who sported tattoos, didn't have a legitimate job (his three different mobile phones gave away what he was really up to), and who bought her a Hervé Léger dress with his spare cash. Kate didn't bat an eyelid. She was used to this sort of treatment. But the previous night, when Zip pushed her and she went flying and ended up with bruises, bumps and a real fear that he would have done something even more crazy if she hadn't fled immediately . . . the next day she decided she was done. Or at least, that's what she told her friends.

She ran down to Bondi Beach, where she knew she'd find Meg and Camilla at their favourite coffee shop. As she sat down, sweaty and feeling accomplished, she drew in a big sigh and announced: 'No more bad boys.'

Meg and Camilla exchanged glances, but nevertheless supported their best friend's decision. After all, they had noticed the bruises on her arm and what looked like bite marks sprinkled in too.

'Cheers to that. We're proud of you,' Camilla said, raising her coffee.

A few days later, as Kate was sitting on her couch contemplating her future, she received a text message from an unknown number.

'I miss you,' it read. Who the hell was this? She grabbed her laptop, flipped it open and Googled the area code. Miami. She didn't know anyone in Miami, except . . .

Troy. And Troy was bad news. Worse than the rest—not because he'd given her her first taste of drugs, but because he really had captured her heart. And while he had abandoned her suddenly during their three-year courtship without a word of goodbye to make the move overseas, Kate never forgot him.

'He says he wants to marry me,' Kate told Camilla over the phone after speaking to Troy. Troy had been the love of her life and a raging alcoholic. He'd left the city to better himself, and escape the debt he'd gotten himself into. A pity he was sixteen hours away. 'I'm going to go and find him and bring him back.'

'It's not a good idea, Kate,' Camilla begged her friend. 'He's only going to do it again.'

'Promise me you'll let me go,' Kate replied softly. 'I need to do this for myself.'

Camilla had no choice.

When Camilla picked up Kate from the airport on her return from Miami, she hardly recognised her gorgeous friend. Kate—usually voluptuously sexy—was gaunt, with ripped, dirty clothes, chipped nails and no make-up except the black mascara running down her face. Camilla knew it was over. She didn't know whether to laugh or cry for Kate. But Kate wasn't in the mood for frivolities.

'I'm done,' Kate said matter-of-factly. 'Take me home.'

Camilla hugged her best friend, feeling her pain.

'We'll get you through this.'

4

But how can I ever view myself as The Catch if I've been dumped?

Before we get into the 30-Day Catch Boot Camp, you are probably thinking to yourself that if you were such a Catch, why won't some guy who you recently dated, slept with or was in a relationship with, call you, date you or beg for you back, right? Well firstly, remember that there was a reason—other than yourself—why the relationship broke up. Most likely it was because you were *incompatible*—not that he found someone better than you.

I had friends constantly reminding me why Mr Ex and I broke up. I kept forgetting. It's a good idea to ask your girlfriends to remind you of the qualities your ex possessed that made you break up with him in the first place.

'But he's so hot!' just isn't going to cut it. That's not a reason to get back together. I'll say it again: you were incompatible. Also, the best advice I can give in the entire world is: *Let go of thoughts that you are ever going to get back together.* Let. It. Go. Seriously. Just stop. Think of him as a good mate who you can have a great conversation with, and make sure that there is no ulterior motive.

Every time I used to catch up with my ex, I did it with the hope that we'd get back together. I used to wear my favourite outfits and get my hair done and, after a few drinks or a few minutes of conversation, I'd casually let it slip that I wanted him back. He'd look at me, sigh, and then tell me that it was not going to happen. 'We're too different,' he'd say.

'But everyone is different!' I'd yell back. 'I'll do anything to make it work!'

I'd break down—and hate myself for doing it. I felt like I wasn't good enough for him. I felt like my whole world would collapse if I wasn't with him. And then one day, I just decided to stop doing it. I decided not to bring it up with him and not to have any expectations of him. I decided that the less I said about it, the more affection he would have towards me. And the more powerful I felt within myself.

The more I let go, the more other men became drawn to me. And suddenly I had a gaggle of men all vying for my attention. And they took up more of my brain space than he did. And then I would see him and it was just like I was seeing a friend. Or a brother. We would hug and talk and laugh—but I was so excited to get back to my own wonderful life after we parted that he no longer affected me. And this was the biggest power of all.

That said, if you are in a position where you strongly believe you are going to get back together (and let me preface this by saying the only way to stay sane is to have no expectations!) then here's the thing: if it's going to happen, it will. *But* you need to give it space and time to happen. Don't force it, don't push it, and know that the more you tell him that you guys are going to have to get back together because you *love* him, the worse things are going to get between you.

Let's talk a little about his attitude after your break-up.

The male break-up brain

When Jackie and Bob called it quits after five years and almost walking down the aisle together, Jackie couldn't understand Bob's actions. It had been less than twenty-four hours after their break-up when Bob had gone out with his mates, got drunk and flirted with other women. She had his Facebook password and checked his page the following night, only to discover that he was already asking out other women. And they were saying yes!

'Isn't he sad about all this?' she cried to me. 'Did I mean nothing to him?'

Well, it did mean something. But the truth is that men process break-ups entirely differently to women.

If it comes as a shock to him and is sudden and quick, then he doesn't feel anything for months on end. He simply goes into autopilot and gets back to his caveman roots: drinking and sex are all that is on his mind.

If, on the other hand, it was his decision, then you can bet he's been thinking about it for a mighty long time and simply hasn't known what to do about it. That's right: men decide *long* before they make the break that they are over a girl. The break-up might come suddenly to you but to him it's been brewing for quite some time. In fact he decided, possibly months ago, that he no longer wanted to be with you. And every day that passed since then, he's felt less and less for you.

I've seen it happen: guy dates girl; guy gets bored with girl; guy waits until girl gets more and more clingy, needy, annoying, and further and further away from the girl he first fell in love with. And then guy dumps girl. Girl is astounded: *How could he have done this? What's wrong with me? Is he* serious? Oh boy, is he *ever*. And now there's absolutely nothing that you can do or say to change his mind—he made it up months ago. And every action of yours since then has been confirming what he had already decided: that you're just not the girl for him.

So unfortunately, you have to accept the break-up. You cannot beg him to take you back. You cannot tell him he's made the biggest mistake of his life. And you cannot bring on his loneliness.

Let's get to the second point of the male break-up brain: yearning for you.

Men have a delayed reaction to the break-up

You know that rush of emotions that women feel when they go through a tough break-up? Blokes don't feel it right away. Something strange happens inside their brains. They go on hold. They put a pause on their emotions. They take a hiatus from their feelings. They put you in a box and lock it up in their closet.

Instead of staying at home with a DVD and a tub of cookies and cream ice-cream, they ring up their mates (who are intoxicatingly happy that their 'bro' is back on the market as their wing man) and they all go out, drink beers, watch the footy and talk about picking up other chicks. To you—in mourning and incredibly depressed and feeling like your life as you know it has come to a screeching halt—this behaviour is utterly mortifying. How dare he enjoy himself! How dare he go out and have fun! How dare he have actual friends! *What the?!*

Don't be too alarmed. This is a man's way of dealing with traumatic events such as break-ups. His real reaction to the break-up is never immediate. It can take months, sometimes even years (it took my Mr Ex one whole year to get back to me about his thoughts on the break-up) for them to admit they feel upset by it, or to reveal their reasoning behind their actions.

For some men (a select few), it may take a few days for them to come crawling back. The key here is not to do anything irrational in the first few days, and to simply allow him to come back to you in his own time. You need to get him thinking about you in the way he thought about you when you first got together: that you are The Catch. And he is still the one who has to chase. No scary girl behaviour in sight. This is where most women go wrong. Scary girl behaviour is what deters even the most in-love man. Don't be that girl.

Crying on the phone to him is not the way to get him back. Crying to your girlfriends (whom you trust) and then putting on a brave face in public is the only way. Telling people who are near to him that you can't live without him—mistake. Telling people near to him that you are doing fine and that you're focusing on your career—the way to do it.

#26. HE MIGHT MOVE ON STRAIGHTAWAY

If he does, do not be bitter or feel like you were traded in for someone better, prettier, whatever . . . instead know that *he* wasn't the right guy for you and that—lucky you— you have a better chance at life . . . and love. A new chance. Not many people get given a second chance. In fact, many people I know are stuck in unhappy relationships.

Never become needy with him — he won't be needy with you

Men are different to you. They don't actually need women. They have porn, they have masturbation, they have their mates, their sport, their beers and they always have wing men to keep them company and to continually impress upon them that it's *so* much better to be a single man than it is to be in a relationship. Of course the reason you're reading this book is because single life is not for you. You want to get back out there, to find someone else. And therefore you have to rebuild your life and yourself in order to do so.

Getting over Bad Boys

The trouble with a Bad Boy addiction is that when you are afflicted with it, you will subconsciously draw Bad Boys into your life. Even if you think that the one you've chosen isn't a Bad Boy, eventually you will discover something about him that proves otherwise. It's an addiction as well as an indication of your state of mind. The way to change it? Going cold turkey on men altogether, and then learning to trust that safe, secure, kind, real men are not going to hurt you. That there really are good guys out there and that there is someone who you will be able to trust and rely on. Aside from the excitement factor, girls become infatuated with bad boys because they rationalise that all men will end up hurting them anyway, so they might as well pick one who is exciting, dangerous and lives life on the edge. It's a terrible spiral that only goes one way: downhill.

My girlfriend Trish worked out how to combat her addiction after much trial and error. After dating Bad Boy after Bad Boy, she eventually realised that she could no longer let herself go on like that. 'Surely I am worthy of a nice guy!' she told me. Then she quit dating altogether, deleted their numbers from her phone and refused to take any dates until she was sure she had built up enough self-esteem and a sense of self-worth so that she could prove to herself that she was indeed deserving of a beautiful, healthy relationship.

While not everyone has to embark on a lengthy detox, in a bid to score the ultimate answers to the Bad Boy dilemma, I contacted Kristina Grish in New York, author of *Addickted: 12 steps to kicking your bad boy habit*.[2] She has formulated a twelve-step recovery program to kicking the addiction to your ex for good. So if you're one of those women with a Bad Boy addiction, read on.

Me: What types of women are addicted to bad men?

Kristina: They're women who are obsessed with erratic charm and tousled bed head—but have no clue about how to alter their destructive dating patterns. In their hearts, they want to adore a prince and know they deserve nothing less, but they also have no clue about

how to transition from devouring one type
to embracing another. They've worked hard
to learn how to deal with and romanticise
wayward trappings—and dating outside this
world demands a serious paradigm shift.
Most sensible women know they won't
spend forever with an attractively damaged
man, but they never cease to sneak one
into their circle—falling harder and unfortunately becoming more hurt with each
experience.

Me: Is it a real addiction?

Kristina: I'm not a therapist, but it is a really difficult
habit to break—and it requires that women
who date Bad Boys completely redefine
how they think about the men they want to
date and eventually marry. To a great extent,
these men are destructive—and getting past
them requires an entire lifestyle change that
comes from an inability to break a pattern.
What does that sound like to you?

Me: C'mon—do we really need a twelve-step
program to get over them?

Kristina: Twelve steps allow you to self-evaluate so
intensely that you can come away from the
process with a real understanding of what's
important to you in a relationship. You'll
define your priorities more effectively than
when you flippantly say, 'I'll never do that

(or him) again!'—and then rebound a few weeks later.

Me: OK, let's get real here. Can you ever truly go from dating Bad Boys to nice guys?

Kristina: Absolutely. I know many women who have, and I did it myself. I married a nice guy!

Me: OK, so you did it. But won't nice guys seem boring from now on?

Kristina: *No.* An entire history of dating Bad Boys actually helps you appreciate nice guys. Bad men provide a wonderful barometer by which you can judge the nice men in your life. It's all so relative. Nice men sparkle by comparison, but you have to walk far and fast from the bad ones to be ready to embrace the good.

Me: What's your key piece of advice for women in this predicament?

Kristina: Don't settle. A Bad Boy once told me, 'Nice grows on trees.' It's not the most insightful comment, but it's true. There are many more kind men in the world than there are rotten ones, but you certainly shouldn't date or settle down with a man just because he's nice. Be selective from the start because, if you're not, you'll end up right where you started.

Think very carefully to yourself if you want to spend your precious time chasing after a Bad Boy who, at the end of the day, is never going to truly make you happy, satisfied or content. Think carefully if that really is the life you want to lead. If the answer is a resounding no (and it should be!) then you need to work hard at switching your mindset. Get out of the place in your head that tells you that the more of a challenge a man is, and the more excitement he gives you, the better life will be. It won't. It might be exciting for a very brief period of time, but let me assure you that if you want a happy ending with a man who is a good provider, a good father to your kids and an amazing, giving, life-long partner to you, then 'nice' is more important than those crazy ups and downs that the Bad Boy so enjoys dishing up.

A Cautionary Tale: Amanda

Party girls are in hot demand. Washed-up party girls are not. Amanda Potts was once one of those party girls who was so in demand, she was paid thousands of dollars simply to show up at a party, smile for the photographers, drink free champagne and then leave. Oh yes, she was once the most envied party girl in all of the city. Young, sexy, with cascading auburn hair and legs to rival Gisele Bündchen's, she modelled in her spare time, when she wasn't studying fashion design at TAFE.

When she wasn't sleeping with famous male models, musicians, out-of-town celebrities or powerful moguls, she was out partying, indulging in enough alcohol and drugs to rival Lindsay Lohan.

She had everything she'd ever lusted after. Ever since she'd made the move from the country to the city to pursue her dream as a model and designer when she was 17 years old, Amanda had climbed her way up the totem pole as fast as her Christian Louboutins could carry her. She knew it was all about appearances in this town, so she'd promptly dyed her golden locks a bright auburn red and before she knew it, she was sought after as a model, received her first pay cheque, and became hot and in demand by both the industry and the men. Oh boy, the men.

After dating more than her fair share (and it all being chronicled by the local gossip papers), she finally landed her ideal man. His name was J.J. Brentwood—television star extraordinaire, Australia's darling, host of the country's hottest music TV show. She promptly moved into his beachside pad and the two of them were dubbed Australia's answer to the E! Channel's Guiliana and Bill. Amanda was on a mission—no matter what psychological harm it may cause her.

Amanda didn't mind that she was often seen as J.J's handbag. After all, it was nice to have a man to provide endless amounts of money—the minute she earned any of her own, she would spend it. Shoes, handbags, designer clothes, cocktails, bottles of Patrón, extravagant lunches—whatever. And boy did she have expensive taste. Hence she loved having a man on a million-dollar contract to foot all her bills. Even though sometimes he wasn't too pleased about it. And even though he sometimes came home from his long filming hours only to get into a fit of rage over the smallest detail, Amanda simply brushed it off. When we're married everything will change, *she continually told herself.* He's just stressed, that's all! *The headlines about their relationship were anything but lurid. Her career was thriving and when J.J. was in one of his moods, she simply ignored him, or went shopping. Anything was better than her old life. At least that's what she continued to tell herself.*

Finally, she no longer had to put up with taking on odd jobs (which she'd rather never talk about again) to pay for her fabric and manufacturer bills as she started her own fashion line.

What a relief! As she sat on the balcony of her new beachside abode and looked down at her sparkling five-carat

Harry Winston diamond ring, she knew that she'd been right to accept J.J.'s marriage proposal. He'd done it in an idyllic setting in the Maldives—one of their many romantic sojourns together—and she'd instantly said yes. Despite the some-thing that started niggling in the back of her mind, she knew her days as a sought-after party girl were over and, at 30 years old, she wasn't exactly getting any younger. Somehow, saying yes to J.J. seemed like the entirely perfect thing to do . . .

5

The 30-Day Man Hiatus

If ever you find yourself acting too much like the Anti-Catch and constantly being tossed back by the men you're dating, it might be time to go on a 30-Day Man Hiatus. That's right! It's time to go cold turkey if you feel like you're getting stuck in a rut or you find yourself dating the same type of man over and over again. It's time to change your habits and give yourself a new lease on your dating life! For the next thirty days, you are going to learn to be alone, and to fill the void within you that you are clinging to men to fill. You're going to learn to look within, and then you're going to find that you are less appealing to those men who are looking to simply prey on weak women.

When you decide to go on a man hiatus, you are

giving yourself a gift. Because let me assure you that when you are at your low point, men will target you as someone they want to fuck and chuck. And that's when life can get awfully disappointing and depressing and it can wear you down.

So, welcome to thirty days without any dates, casual sex or even talk about boys. Put it all to one side for a minute and start to shift the focus back onto yourself. And believe me, it works. Every woman who has ever taken this 30-Day Man Hiatus, and there have been hundreds so far, has come out the other end stronger and more equipped to meet 'the one'—and many have even found him. So put away your mobile phone, delete your booty call buddies from your speed dial and get ready for thirty man-free days.

You can take on the 30-Day Man Hiatus at any time during your single life. When you feel like things are getting a little too tough and you're constantly being disappointed by the same sorts of men over and over again, stop, take a breather and start to exit stage left. Tell them you're going away. Or better yet, just go away!

So grab a girlfriend (or two) and encourage them to join you on your program. But remember, it is your personal journey to becoming a stronger, more independent, more Catch-worthy woman. So let's get started!

THE CONTRACT

I, _____, hereby solemnly swear to stay off men for the next thirty days. No dates, no sex, no expectations. And I will do my best to attempt to decrease the number of hours I talk about men too.

Signed: _____

Date: _____

The aim

You are to stop letting your life revolve around men, dating and husband hunting, and to get back to your true self—strong, powerful, independent and in demand! You will no longer rely on a man to make you feel good about yourself, to fill in the blanks or to occupy your time when you are uncertain of exactly what to do with yourself. You will learn to love yourself again—just you—and the minute you fall in love with yourself, a man will come along who will be able to fall in love with the new you. Falling in love with yourself takes time, practice, dedication and hard work. But I know you can do it!

The rules

- No dating.
- No online dating.

- No booty calls.
- No casual sex.
- No sex with the ex.
- Delete phone numbers of anyone you think you might be tempted to contact.
- Stop frequenting places where you usually pick up.
- Get yourself a bunch of non-dating wing women and stick with them away from man-friendly destinations.

Week 1

During a man hiatus, it is important that you shift your mindset. You learn to realise that you don't need to get attention from a man in order to feel whole and fulfilled. Instead you are going to learn to do that all on your own. Which means during Week 1, you're going to have to find activities to do that don't involve men.

Avoid late-night texting

The trouble a lot of women find themselves in during the man hiatus is that at night, after they've gone out or gotten home from work, made dinner and watched some television, they start to wonder about what a certain man is up to. And so they decide to text or call him. The response from the man makes them feel instantly good about themselves—it's like an almighty sugar high hits their nervous system and they feel elated, happy and on top of the world.

So, how are you going to get this feeling without a man there to give it to you? Easy. You find something else that is equally fulfilling. But that fulfilling thing is going to have nothing to do with another person making you feel good. It will be something that you *can* control and something that, when you do start dating again, is going to make you interesting, exciting and someone a man wants to get to know better. My favourite suggestions include the following.

Reading inspiring self-help books that aren't about relationships

Aside from reading this book, instead of reading about why a man might not be that into you, or why women talk and men walk, or whatever your latest dating self-help book is called, you are going to switch that for something you are passionate about. That could be a self-help book about starting a small business; being a good business manager; learning how to manage your money better; learning how to run long-distance marathons; learning how to cook. Whatever it might be, its purpose *must* be to enhance you as an individual. This time—which is usually between the hours of 9 pm and 11 pm (the time you are most likely to want to text or receive a text from a man)—will now become about empowering and inspiring yourself. You will turn off your phone (or, if you can't bear the thought, keep it on silent), you will get into bed, play some inspiring, soft music (or loud rap, if you prefer) and you will open up your book. You will make notes, you will think about how you can apply the principles to your everyday life and you will begin to make changes to your life in ways that do not include a man. Who doesn't want to learn how to earn more money, cook better, lose weight, run faster, etc. Yes, it's time to refocus, connect with your inner passions and enhance other parts of yourself.

Reading an autobiography about someone who fascinates you

There are so many amazing stories out there about smart, independent women who made waves in everything from politics to journalism to feminism. Start reading up on the women who might interest you, and enjoy their journeys. Learn from them. Get inspired by them. Recharge your brain, your mind and your soul.

Start enjoying alone time

So what if your phone is running red hot with dates? If they're all below your standards, what the heck is the point? Start reprioritising your goals and getting your life on track the way you want to live it. Become the woman who a man will want to date, not a woman whose sole purpose in life is to snag herself a man. Now that's just weak and, quite frankly, damn boring.

#27. BEING HAPPY WITHOUT A MAN LETS HIM FIND YOU

Men do not complete you. Seriously. Find a hobby. Make some new friends. Find people who inspire you. Find a job that you love and thrive on, one that gives you the same thrill as a date does. Have something of interest to talk about other than men. And don't forget to keep your femininity, your exercise regime and your self-worth up high. Take this time to work on improving yourself. The man will eventually follow.

Other suggestions for things to do while you're on your hiatus:

- Watch arthouse films.
- Visit museums.
- Jump on a ferry.
- Learn a sport.
- Learn to cook.

Start making plans on how to accomplish all these things within the first week of your hiatus. You need to be able to successfully fill up your time with things that replenish you as a person, spiritually, emotionally and academically. Think of all the time you waste on men, and then think about how brilliantly used all that free time could be if you put it into working on your mind.

Week 2

Now that you've got your mind on track, it's time to focus on your body. A hiatus from men also means a hiatus from eating fatty foods just because a man asked you to dinner at a Chinese restaurant. It means not drinking as much as you usually do when you are nervous on a first date and need some liquid courage. And guess what? You are actually waking up every single morning with a clear head—no hangover! So, it's time to get onto the hot water and lemon first thing in the morning, a healthy breakfast, a light lunch and a lovely dinner that you should aim to cook for yourself at least a few times a week. And it's time to get moving. Pick one activity to take up now you have so much free time. It could be Pilates, boxing, tennis, rowing, swimming, skipping—whatever will make you sweat!

Week 3

This is the time to really and truly expand yourself. I want you to take up a hobby. Enrol in a course that interests you; this could be a cooking course, a language course, a course on how to trade shares in the stock market—the choices are endless. One friend on a hiatus took up knitting, another took up art, and another joined a poetry reading group!

Week 4

Go to the movies, get massages, go to the beach, eat great meals and drink cocktails by the sunset. Make a habit of it too. It's the most liberating feeling to discover there's a whole world out there that you can actually enjoy by yourself or with a girlfriend that doesn't *require* a man.

Get a vibrator if you're as horny as hell. Don't see a man as your ticket to an orgasm—most of the time a man isn't one anyway.

End of Week 4

Congratulations! Your man hiatus month is up! You are now free to reply to any of those text messages from men sent to you during your hiatus. You are free to accept dates from men who you might think are worthy of your attentions. You might want to go out with your single girlfriends to a bar or club and actually swap numbers with a cute, eligible bachelor. The world is your oyster. And yet you are so very fulfilled, knowledgeable and fun that men are going to be flocking to you, so you won't even have to do any work! How brilliant is that! The other good thing is that you have successfully managed to do what you set out to before you jumped into the man hiatus—you've fallen in love with yourself. You revel in spending time with yourself and in your own company. You've worked out ways to have a fabulous time without a man involved. You've enriched your mind, body and spirit. You are a Catch now—and nothing is going to stop you!

Part 2

The Single
Catch

❤ ❤

A Cautionary Tale: Camilla

Camilla was determined to not let The Banker get her down. And sure enough, soon after that she met a man: Ryan, a French–Canadian CEO of a major Fortune 100 company. He was sexy, tall and handsome. She was in lust. He didn't exactly court her in the traditional way—more like the odd text message here and there. He didn't exactly make plans to take her out on a date, but was always sure to invite her out after he'd had dinner with his friends; he made sure he bought her drinks and kept in contact with her every few days. Nothing had transpired between them yet, but she certainly enjoyed his company, his sense of adventure, his quick wit and the fact that he was incredibly smart. She also thought he was seriously hot and the chemistry between them was definitely starting to heat up. It was funny but when she first met him, she was a little taken aback by his awkwardness—the way one pant leg had been mistakenly tucked into his sock, the fact that his hair was standing up on end completely unbrushed or tamed, and the way he stood clumsily not knowing where to put his long, gangly arms. But it seemed the more she got to know him, the more into him she became. He was definitely charming, and his geekiness was starting to become endearing, if not incredibly sexy.

It was one of those balmy summer nights and Camilla was at a work function when she received a call from Ryan inviting her to the Ivy for drinks. She immediately rang Kate, who agreed to accompany her friend to meet this Ryan guy she had been hearing so much about.

After they'd downed three rounds of drinks, it was time to leave. Just as they were waiting for a cab outside the restaurant, Ryan pushed Camilla to the side of the entrance behind a big, white billowing curtain and kissed her.

'Want to get a hotel room?' he whispered into her ear.

The words made her nether regions tingle. 'Hell yes.'

Tipsy, filled with confidence and not wearing any under-wear (she'd run out and was too lazy to do any washing), she waved Kate goodbye and followed Ryan into a waiting cab. They made love in an expensive hotel room—seven times. This is the guy I deserve, *Camilla thought. She liked everything about Ryan: his body; his sense of humour; his job; his car; his tanned skin; his sea-green eyes. God, he was cute. And wealthy. And sexy. And a generous lover. Wow!*

The following morning, after they'd shared a breakfast of poached eggs and smoked salmon at the hotel buffet, they sat lounging around by the hotel pool.

Camilla was enjoying every moment as she sat in his arms and he tickled her shoulder. Suddenly he stopped, sat up and looked at her intently.

'Listen,' he began, sounding a little nervous, 'I have two things to tell you.'

Camilla waited in anticipation. Was he going to ask her to move in with him? Be his girlfriend?

'I have a girlfriend,' he was saying.

What the fuck?

'So basically, we are two consenting adults who decided to have sex. But we can't speak in public, OK?'

Another pause.

'Oh, and the other thing . . .' he continued, still brushing her shoulder, 'the condom broke last night. Can you get the morning after pill?'

Camilla was astonished. 'Well, I have a boyfriend too! So don't worry about it!' she lied, feeling sick to her stomach. She hoped her face didn't give away her disappointment.

'I need a vodka, now,' was all Camilla could say as she arrived at Kate's house that morning, dishevelled, still drunk and looking a little worse for wear. 'Why did you let me go home with him?'

'Girl, there was nothing—not even me—that was going to stop you last night. Anyhoo . . . Grey Goose and lemon coming right up!' Kate said.

Cam slept on Kate's couch for three nights in a row, drinking Grey Goose.

With the help of Kate, she found a small, dingy apartment nearby to rent for a few months. Not wanting to be there much, she threw herself into her work. There just didn't seem to be any other option. Yes, she'd work as hard as she could and forget about men altogether.

And just when she was at her most vulnerable, she met Nate.

Nate attended a work function as a guest of one of Camilla's colleagues, while the colleague's husband was out of town, *and the minute Camilla laid eyes on him, the chemistry was palpable. They'd left the party together for a late-night snack. And since then, Camilla couldn't get him out of her mind. So when he asked her out on a date a few nights later, she couldn't resist.*

She had a spray tan, bought a new dress (and maxed out her credit card) and did her make-up in that 'I'm not wearing any make-up' way because Nate told her he liked women who looked natural. As she rode down in the lift, she felt butterflies. Why did he make her so nervous?

'You look very pretty tonight, Milly,' he said, kissing her on the cheek as she got into his Jeep. She giggled.

'You look very handsome indeed,' she replied, taking in his skinny jeans, motorcycle boots, icy blue eyes and T-shirt that set his eyes off just enough to make him look sexy and relaxed all at the same time. I am so lucky to be with the hottest man on the planet! *she thought happily.*

'So where are we going?'

He took her to this way-out sushi restaurant where a jazz band was playing in the background.

'We'll order everything!' he announced to the waitress. And then dropped his voice to a whisper. 'By the way, you are the prettiest waitress I've ever seen,' he said to the plumpish girl who had a curly mop of brown hair and wore way too much orange bronzer.

'Thank you,' she said, blushing. As she walked away giggling, Camilla noticed her glance back at Nate. The waitress must have been the happiest she'd been in years, because throughout the night she couldn't stop staring at their table,

looking for Nate's approval, which he gave her every time she came by. God, he is so sweet, *thought Camilla.* What a gentleman. So nice . . .

They ate, and talked about everything. He asked her about her family, how it was growing up, what her goals and aspirations were for her life. He was so interested in everything about her that it made her feel like a giddy little schoolgirl.

Finally! Camilla was so relieved to finally be in a relationship again. When they weren't together, however, Nate acted a little odd. He was never available when she called him, and he never scheduled dates ahead of time. They were always spontaneous. Texts here and there when she least expected them, asking if they could meet up right that minute. Not that she minded. She was head over heels for him and he was the perfect Catch. He was smart, good-looking, had a great job and was charming, funny and, above all, he doted on Camilla. And he hadn't even pressured her for sex yet! What a change in pace, she thought happily as she drifted off to sleep.

A few weeks later, Kate scheduled an emergency meeting with Camilla. They were sitting at their favourite table at Toko—right in the centre of the room—where all the men walking in and out were able to spot the gorgeous twosome. Camilla loved being friends with Kate because whenever Kate was in a room, all the men would gawk and stare at the two of them. And the best part was that not only did the two best friends not have the same taste in men at all, but usually out of a group of guys, there would be at least one who was only into blondes.

So even though Camilla always let Kate walk first into a room, she knew that when all the men turned, there would be one who would see Camilla trailing behind and decide that she was his because brunettes just weren't his thing. It was genius. Yes, Kate was the best wing woman on the planet, and Camilla loved milking every second of being best friends with the gorgeous brunette.

'I need to tell you something,' Kate said quietly, sipping on her peach bellini. The bellinis were genius at Toko. It was enough to make anyone as happy as a newly engaged spinster—even if the bellinis cost half of Camilla's weekly wage.

'There's something about Nate I need to tell you,' Kate said. 'And I need you to listen to me, OK?'

Camilla nodded. Ah, Nate. The very mention of his name . . .

'There was this girl who came in to get a facial the other day. And she was gushing about her engagement ring and how in love she was with this guy.'

'Oh that's so cool!' Camilla said, sipping her drink, dreaming of the previous night she'd spent with Nate. God, he was a good kisser. Sure, they hadn't slept together yet, but she thought it was kind of cute that they were waiting anyway. So romantic! No guys ever waited any more! She knew that he was aware she was desperate to do it with him. She often hinted at how much she wanted it, but he always told her that they should wait. She wasn't exactly sure how much longer she could hold out for . . .

'No, Cam, you're not listening to me. She was saying how they dated when they were in high school, and a few *months ago, she decided that she didn't want to be single any more, so she called him up and they got back together. And how he's always been in love with her, and that she was so excited when he agreed to see her. She showed me a photo on her iPhone of the two of them at her parents' house in Palm Beach this weekend. And it was him. It was a photo of Nate.'*

Suddenly Camilla went cold. The bellini curdled in her stomach and she had a sudden urge to go and throw up.

'Hello? Say something, Cam. I'm so sorry.'

'Just give me a few moments,' Camilla replied. She wasn't exactly sure what to say or do next. She needed to think about this. To work out if it was true.

'Who—who is she?'

'Well, here's the thing . . .' Kate's voice trailed off.

'Kate—who the fuck is she? Tell me now!' Camilla was hysterical.

'Shhh . . . people are starting to stare. OK, OK. Listen, they went to high school together. It's that socialite girl he used to date . . . Kathryn something.'

Camilla swallowed hard. Things were suddenly starting to make a hell of a lot of sense. The disappearing acts; the fact he didn't want to sleep with her. She thought back to how he had courted her: invited her out for a drink, kissed her that night, called her a few days later, asked her out for dinner; constantly keeping her on her toes.

Camilla hadn't been able to get off the couch for days. Her routine was simple: wake up feeling like death; pop a Xanax;

lie down again; listen to music; turn it off because it was too depressing; try to eat; think of throwing up. Until one day, the girls staged an intervention.

'Babe, this behaviour is crazy,' Kate said softly, with Meg and Amanda by her side. 'You need to get over it and move on with your life. These guys are not worth it. Not worthy of you. Please.'

'No, I'm not moving,' Camilla said. She'd tried her best. She was putting herself out there and all she was getting back was crap. The fake banker, the CEO and now this? And with that thought she closed her eyes, and tried to shut out the world.

Cam sank deeper and deeper into depression. Every morning she'd wake up and wish that her Big Break-up was all just a horrible dream. That she was back in the apartment she had shared with Mr Ex and that she was in his arms again. She didn't give a fuck how skinny his arms were any more. At least those arms had loved her. At least they didn't lie to her. At least he was safe, secure and he loved her whether she had a pimple on her forehead or a few extra kilos on her thighs. He didn't give a toss. They were an item. They were soul mates. They were destined to get married. So what the fuck happened?

It was late and the buzzer rang at her apartment. Strange. She picked up the receiver to see who it was.

'Cam?'

It was Nate. She threw on her favourite oversized T-shirt emblazoned with gold studs and her denim shorts and opened the door.

'Hi.'

'Nate, I can't do this any more,' she said, tearing up. 'I know you're engaged.'

'Do you think I led you on?' he said.

Led her on? Was he fucking joking? She didn't want to give the douchebag the satisfaction.

'Well, no.'

'Listen, Milly, I never expected to meet anyone like you. Girls like you only come around every five, maybe ten years in a guy's life.'

She wanted to scream back at him: So fucking what? She knew she was a Catch and had simply fallen for his bullshit games. And now she was standing in front of him, having to listen to more of his stupid lies.

'You lied to me, Nate. I don't want to see you any more. I can't. How can I be the one doing that to another woman? How can I be seeing a guy who has a fiancé? It's not right— for her sake. I just can't do it. Even though I like you, it's tough.'

'I don't want to hear this. I'm leaving,' he said.

'What? Now you expect me to follow you out?'

'No. I just need to go home. Be alone.'

And with that he walked out of her door, and out of her life.

6

The male response to The Catch

How your man *should* react when you're The Catch

Once you reach Catch status, you will no longer have to do anything. That's right—you will have to do absolutely nothing. Ever. He will organise dates, make plans, call you, text you, want to woo you and want to be in contact with you. And the best part is that if he stops contacting you for whatever reason, you are so busy with your wonderful life you will hardly even notice he hasn't contacted you. As The Catch you also have an understanding that there will be times when the man you are dating needs time to process you. Even if he is completely into you, the male natural instinct is to delay his timeline and take the proper time to figure things out in his mind.

You also know that by doing anything at all—in terms of contacting him during this phase or asking him why he has been distant—will only serve to bite you in the butt. If you try to make his decision for him, he will retreat from you and no decision will be made at all.

#28. MEN NEED TO PURSUE YOU: THE MALE SEXUAL PURSUIT GENE

According to brain expert Louann Brizendine, the 'sexual pursuit' area of the male brain is two and a half times larger than it is in the female brain, which means all men want to pursue women.[3] Give to him (anything!) and you'll ruin his enjoyment in the pursuit. He'll give up and find someone more challenging to pursue. The Catch always makes her boyfriend think he is still pursuing, even long after her heart has been caught.

Make it easy for him and he'll put you into the 'cheap and quick' category. And he'll just as quickly (and cheaply) give you the flick once he's done.

How the Chase Gene works without you having to do anything

Karen, a 28-year-old single girl, went to a dinner with a group for a mutual friend's birthday. Patty—the same age as Karen—was there too. A gorgeous-looking man sat at the table next to Karen. Karen now sat between him and Patty.

'Hi, I'm Shane,' the man introduced himself to Karen, extending a tanned, buff arm.

'Hey, I'm Patty!' the other woman squealed in excitement, leaning over Karen to shake Shane's hand. 'Tell me all about yourself, Shane!'

This made Karen uncomfortable and so she offered to swap seats with Patty. 'Thank you so much, babe! I'd love to!'

Patty turned her back to Karen and regaled Shane with stories about her life, her dating history, her sexual escapades and her latest work projects.

Karen didn't know many other people at the dinner table and so after an hour or so, she decided to leave.

'You're leaving already?' Shane asked Karen, surprised. 'OK, well I'll find you on Facebook!'

The following day, Shane kept his word. He did find Karen on Facebook. He even got her number from the mutual friend whose birthday dinner it had been. He then called to ask Karen out.

Patty was mortified. 'But Karen didn't even speak to him!' she told their mutual friend. 'I did! *I* was speaking to him the whole night! I'm sure he made a mistake!'

'Yes, but Karen acted like a lady,' said their mutual friend. She sure did. Karen and Shane dated, and Karen couldn't believe her luck. He was charming, good-looking and dynamite in the sack.

When Patty called Karen to question her about Shane, Karen simply said: 'If you like a guy, ignore him, Patty. Men work on their biological urge to chase. You don't offer yourself to a man on a platter.'

But Karen hadn't known this when she left the dinner party the night she met Shane. After they'd been dating for a few weeks, he told her how he thought she was hard to get. How he'd had to call someone to get her phone number. How he was surprised that she wasn't interested in him and that she hadn't attempted to impress him at the dinner table like so many other women usually did. After all, he knew he was a Catch. But Karen knew her worth too. She valued herself as a Catch, and he sensed it . . . and he decided that even though she didn't speak to him that night, she was something special.

A wise woman once told me that if you like a man, ignore him. Let's take a look at Karen's behaviour with Shane. She met him, liked what she saw and realised that if she was going to ascertain whether or not he was *really* interested in her, she was going to have to ignore him. Easy. No effort necessary. Patty, on the other hand, mistakenly believed that the more she talks to, hangs around and flirts with a man, the more he's going to fall in love with her. Not true. When Shane saw Karen, he liked what he saw too. And when she left the party abruptly, he asked their friend for Karen's number. And when he asked her out on a date, and she didn't let him up to her apartment, he was even more intrigued.

'This woman was different,' he told me when I asked him what had transpired. 'My interest was piqued when she left the party. And on our first date I could tell she didn't just want sex.'

It was hard for Shane to fathom why a woman would act so uninterested in him. After all, he was used to women falling all over him, inviting him up to their apartments on the first date and willing him into sex. Then he'd get bored and swiftly move on. But with Karen it was different. Why? Karen had become a 'strong woman'—who didn't wait around for a man.

Karen's new motto was: 'If he's interested, he'll show me. If he's not he won't. That way I won't waste my time with men who aren't.'

What this does is weed out all the men who aren't suitable for you anyway. Let's be honest here—why would you want to be with a dude who only half likes you because you chewed his ear off about all your accomplishments? I mean, seriously? Not Karen. She'd learned that the less you say and do, the better your chances are of meeting a quality guy and weeding out the ones who sort of feel forced into a romantic interlude with you.

#29. IF YOU LIKE A GUY, IGNORE HIM

Talking to a man about yourself for hours on end isn't going to make him like you more. It's the woman who walks away or has other things to do who is the one he becomes intrigued with and eager to chase.

If he's not persisting, he's not 'just shy'

Of course there are times when you meet a man who is so shy he's got no idea how to talk to women and so he simply gives up—unless she chases him. Well, you've got to decide for yourself if he's really 'shy'—and doesn't actually have the Chase Gene—or if he's just not interested. Because mostly, he's just not that interested. And even if he is, are you going to be waiting on your toes every weekend for him to get up the courage to call or text you? Bullshit. I'm sorry, but no matter what women like to peddle to one another, every man has a Chase Gene. If it doesn't set in when you meet him, *ignore him*.

The Chase Gene

While a man you fancy might have the Chase Gene in the early stages of dating, what you do with it is extremely important. It's imperative that you do not play games, but if you are actually busy, you do not stop what you are doing and text him right away. Nor do you give yourself up on a platter too easily. But you know that by now.

The reason I'm telling you about this Chase Gene isn't so that you can take advantage of it, but so you can take the pressure of trying to impress him off yourself, or thinking of every guy you meet as the potential 'one' upon first meeting. Let him show his cards. Get to know him. Let *him* impress *you*—not the other way around.

Too often women decide when they like a guy that they need to impress him. So they organise dates, regale him with their achievements, show off to him about their success or the amount of money they have or how fast they can run—whatever. The fact is that when men like a woman, they want to be the ones trying to impress her. And here's how their minds work: the more they *feel* they have to work to get a woman's affection, the more they trick themselves into liking her.

Unlike women, men feel that the more they need to work for your affections, the more important you are to them. So often women mistake this behaviour for something else. Instead of simply saying 'thank you' and being appreciative, they feel as though they have to give back in the early stages of dating. This isn't so. In fact, men are hardwired to do as much as they can to impress you in the early stages of pursuit. So he plans dates, pays for things, tells you what you want to hear and doesn't expect anything in return other than your appreciation.

What he is really trying to ascertain is how much of a Catch he thinks you are. And the more you appreciate his gestures and encourage him to plan more things and to give more, the more he thinks that he must be doing all these things for a woman because she must be a Catch. It's like his actions are tricking his mind into thinking more highly of you. And the bonus—you don't have to do anything at all but enjoy them!

#30.   **THE MORE A MAN GIVES TO YOU, THE MORE HE LIKES YOU**

This might seem counter-intuitive. You might feel like you have to give back to him since he's given up so much for you. But the fact is you don't. In his attempt to work out how much of a Catch you are, he wants to see how much he's willing to give to ascertain how important you are to his subconscious mind.

Allowing a man to take the lead in the dating process and to do things for you, plan dates, woo you and get you to like him is wonderful. And how easy is that? But here's the caveat: do not let your timeline trump all this hard work. Do not let your Female Urge to Rush Things get in the way of him pursuing you and working out whether or not you're the Catch. You are—and he will believe that you are—if you just let his timeline do its thing for at least *three to four months*.

A Cautionary Tale: Camilla

A few weeks after she'd last seen Nate, Camilla sat up all night Googling the word 'players'. She wanted to get inside their heads, to understand why they do the things they do. She still couldn't understand why Nate would do that. Why anyone would do something like that? What was his game? Get a girl to fall in love with him so he can fuck her over? What was the point? Was she still being punished for her bust-up with her Mr Ex? Was this how all men were going to behave from here on in?

No man will ever love me like Mr Ex did, *she thought.*

Why didn't she have another boyfriend yet? What was wrong with her? Why didn't any guys want to chase her; to love, support, give her what she needed? Was she choosing the wrong men? Was she doing something wrong? Did she have to lower her standards? Or lift them? She was determined not to get back into her funk. To not have to rely on guys like Nate. Or her ex. Or anyone. She would have to be happy on her own.

Camilla finally pulled it together about a fortnight later. She was about to embark on a new life in a new job at a twenty-four-hour news television station as their hot new political reporter.

As she was walking to work one day, she noticed a bunch of people leaving a gym. She took a peek inside: there was a boxing ring and several boxing bags. Exactly what she needed.

'Where do I sign up?' she asked at the front desk.

'Over here, sugar,' replied a burly, muscular man who looked like he spent every waking hour doing bench presses.

And so she did. Every day, during her lunch break, she would hit the boxing ring. The more she went and the harder she punched, the stronger she felt herself getting. Each day was a healing process. Each minute was like the best sort of therapy money could buy.

'Fuck him. Fuck Mr Ex. Fuck all exes!' She punched harder and harder. She was toning up, and fast. She noticed new ab definition. She noticed her arms were building up. She was fitter and stronger than ever before. She was ready to take on the world. And nothing was going to stop her. There weren't any men texting her. None were calling her. There weren't any on rotation. And she kind of liked it that way. Suddenly she was enjoying life just the way it was. And it was surprisingly kind of peaceful.

A Cautionary Tale: Kate

'I think I need to start dating again,' Kate told Camilla. Camilla was sitting in the waiting room at Kate's beauty salon, flipping through a magazine. Camilla loved her monthly visits and felt blessed that her best friend was the facialist to the stars. Not to mention the fact that Kate was incredibly gifted with her fingers. Hence Camilla (and every other gal in the city) raced into her salon to have Kate work her magic on her skin. Today was the first day in a long time that Kate was in surprisingly good spirits.

'And I'm definitely over my bad-boy phase,' Kate announced, clicking her tongue as though it was a done deal. 'Yep. No more bad boys, drug addicts, abusers or controlling men. Over it, done—I'm ready to find myself a normal guy with no issues or criminal records.'

It was about time too. At 35 years old, she'd spent way too long rotating through super bad boys and getting involved in relationships which were definitely going nowhere fast. As long as she felt in the danger zone, she was happy. But that was then. She could feel there was a change in the air, and she was excited about what the future would hold.

'Hello? Delivery for Kate?' A small woman was standing at the door of the salon with the most magnificent bunch of white lilies the girls had ever seen.

'Who are these from?' Kate asked, ecstatically grabbing the card that was attached to the bunch.

The woman pointed across the road to an office building. Kate eagerly opened the envelope containing the note. There were six words: 'Go on a date with me?'

There was no name!

Kate tried to ignore the flowers. She did, however, secretly wonder who the man behind them was, and what it might be like to date him. A few days later there was a knock on her salon door. When she opened it, there stood a tall, blue-eyed man with rugged hair. She'd definitely seen him walking around the area before, and while she had certainly noticed him thanks to his being tall, dark and handsome, she'd never paid him much attention. She was usually too busy chasing the bad boys to notice anyone else.

'Hey, I'm Joe. I see you liked the flowers?' *He pointed to the blooms that sat on her desk.*

'Oh, those were from you? Yes, thank you so much!'

'So, what was your answer?'

'To what question?'

'The one on the card? Just one drink, that's all I ask,' *he said, smiling. He looked so innocent and sweet—unlike the usual slew of bad boys that she'd dated. But she wasn't quite sure she was ready . . .*

What the hell? It was just one drink. 'OK, how about tonight?' *she said.*

But that night, Kate didn't make it. She had to work back and by the time she'd locked up it was way too late for a first date. The next time he asked her out, she was sick and ended up in bed. On the weekend she had an out-of-town wedding. The following week she was so busy with work that she barely had time to call her best friends, let alone share a drink with a stranger. Finally, Joe wouldn't stand any more rejection.

'It's on tonight or I'm going to have to stop chasing you,' he said.

'All right. Tonight, I promise.'

Usually Kate changed her outfit at least five times before a date. But this time she wasn't in the mood. She was very much over men. Over all the drama. She didn't give a shit about getting married or having a future with any of them. Fuck 'em. What was the fucking point? she wondered. They all just ended up disappointing her anyway.

Yet even despite her exasperation with men, she'd nevertheless acquiesced to a date tonight. After all, dating was a rather new concept to her. Sure, she was one of those women who had a constant gaggle of men all begging for her attention, and many of them for her hand in marriage. She was exceptionally beautiful—statuesque with long hair cascading down to her butt, topped with exotically made-up chocolate

---

#31. SOMETIMES YOU NEED TO THROW OUT YOUR CHECKLIST

When a man who isn't your usual type pursues you, it's important you give him the chance he deserves. Sometimes you might be pleasantly surprised—and discover that what you thought you wanted wasn't actually what you wanted at all.

eyes and voluptuous lips that made any man quiver with anticipation.

'So, Joey,' Kate said belligerently to the guy sitting opposite her at the garden restaurant he'd picked for their date. 'Why do you keep chasing me when I've said no to a date with you, like, a hundred times?' She had demolished half a bottle of wine, picked at some lettuce leaves in her salad, and was now staring at him and wondering what the hell was wrong with him. Thoughts were ricocheting through her head. There must be something, *she thought. After all, there was usually something wrong with guys who were attracted to her—deep-seated issues which quickly emerged after the first few dates. She knew how to attract the crazies, that was for sure. There was the drug addict, the drug dealer, the liar and the player. And right now, she was wondering exactly what was Joey's big problem.*

'Because I like you,' he replied, looking at her squarely in the eye. He didn't seem afraid of her like all the other guys seemed to be. And she kind of liked it. Who is this guy? *she wondered. He didn't look very old either. Maybe 26 or 27? Still, he had an air of confidence about him. He seemed mature. Like he could take on anything. Not like the immature 30-somethings she usually dated.*

'And what do you like about me?' she asked, looking at him intently. 'You don't even know me, so it's got to be my tits, right?'

Joey didn't back down. 'Well, I've actually been watching you from across the road for months now.' He paused, and when she didn't bite back, he continued: 'I can see the way you are with your clients. You're so gentle. So giving. You have a little bit of sadness in your eyes that I notice every now and again. But you hide it so well. Everyone seems to love and admire you. And you always look so beautiful. No matter if it's at the beginning of the day or the end of the week.'

Damn. No man had ever spoken to her like that. What was this guy's problem? Did he not know how much trouble she was?

'So Joey . . .' She paused, taking another sip of the fresh glass of wine the waiter had just poured for her. 'How old are you?'

'I'm 24.'

Kate choked on her wine.

'What!'

'Yeah. People say I look a bit older. Why, how old are you? Twenty-five?'

Kate let out a cackling laugh.

'Let's just say I might actually be a little older than you. Oh, maybe like a decade older. We'd never work, so we might as well not even bother.'

She glanced at Joey, and noticed his smile was even wider than ever before.

'What do you have to lose?' he said, with a glint in his eye. He gently touched her face. And then he leaned in and kissed her.

Boy, am I in trouble, *she thought.*

7

The 30-Day Catch Boot Camp

Aim: To turn from a woman men view as weak and not confident—a Toss—into a strong woman who will only attract the highest calibre of male who is worthy of your time—a Catch. You will never chase another man again and instead have a gaggle of guys all attempting to pin you down.

Duration: Thirty days.

Contract: I, _____, hereby declare that for an entire month, I will do everything I can to turn me into a strong woman. I will stop and think about all my actions before I complete them and ask myself, 'Does this make me stronger?'

If the answer is no, I will refrain from doing it.
This includes:

- Not giving time to men who aren't worthy of me
- Engaging in activities on a daily basis that make me stronger both mentally and physically
- Avoiding all negative self-talk
- Learning to enjoy alone time
- Never waiting around for a man to text or call me
- Refusing to get depressed over the lack of a boyfriend in my life
- Fostering friendships, relationships and a career that empowers me
- Telling myself every single day that I am a strong woman.

I hereby agree that by signing this contract, I am beginning my thirty days of this challenge in order to become a stronger, more confident woman who doesn't rely on a man to make me feel that way.

Signed: _____
Date: _____

Thirty days to a stronger you

Thirty days. That's all I ask of you. But I want to let you in on a little secret: becoming a strong woman doesn't just last you thirty days. It lasts a lifetime. Hence it will be the best 30-day investment you ever made. So let's get started. To become a Catch, you need to be a strong woman. So first, let's define exactly what a strong woman is:

Strong woman (n.): A strong woman is strong mentally, physically and emotionally and knows *exactly* who she is. She is able to live on her own without a man and is never desperate, needy or accepting of a man's scraps. The strong woman is never obsessed with any man, doesn't beg for her ex to take her back and is never sitting around waiting for a man to call her—she has better things to do. The strong woman attracts only the strongest, best man to be her partner. And she knows and appreciates him when he comes along.

The strong woman is one who emanates an energy so powerful she draws men to her by kicking their Chase Gene into gear. How does she do this? By the way she walks, what she believes, how she sees herself and the way her inner strength has the ability to emanate from her every thought, word and action. I once told a girlfriend—who hadn't been asked out on a date in three years, let alone gotten laid—that you have to fake it till you make it. So what if you think you're too fat or too dumb or not good enough for a man? Believe you are good enough. Believe that you are worthy of being chased. And watch the magic happen.

Plus, the stronger you become, the more you stop taking shit from guys. The more you stop taking shit, the more you stop attracting douchebags and arseholes. The quicker you do that, the quicker you leave room for Mr Wonderful to waltz into your life. And the better he will be because he will hunt and chase you down because you're The Catch. And the less time you'll spend having those stupid conversations in your head where you ask if you are good enough for this man. Because, quite frankly, you are now wondering if *he* is good enough for you—and you're allowing him the *time* and *space* to prove it.

Why you need to take this challenge

When I was at my lowest point, I knew that there was no way in hell I was going to meet a decent guy. What man would want to enter that world? None. I was also dating *way* below my standards and I would try so desperately to impress every man I met that they would sense my desperation and run a mile. So I decided to make the switch from being a weak woman to a strong one. It took a lot of might to do so—a lot of personal work and figuring out who I was. But in the end it was worth it. Also, know that the process of becoming a strong woman is a powerful time in your life. There will be tears, loneliness, happiness, fulfilment, regret, remorse . . . Let yourself feel all of it. Go through it like you're walking through a thick black cloud that you know has a rainbow at the end of it. So just enjoy the journey as much as you can. You will never have this time in your life again to just be.

Week 1: Reading about something that fascinates men

This is one of my favourite things to do whether I am on a boot camp or not. Because the trick here is that you are seriously expanding your mind, while at the same time gaining some awesome arsenal to charm a man once your boot camp is over. Men are obsessed with sport, business, gangs, banks, war . . . you get the drift. It might sound boring to you right now, but I guarantee you that if you pick up a book like *Confessions of the Wolf of Wall Street* by Jordan Belfort or *Too Big to Fail* by Andrew Ross Sorkin, the amount of knowledge you gain about the financial industry from these books will be unparalleled. It's interesting, it's intriguing, it's fascinating and it's something that other women often don't take the time to learn, which means that when you meet a man, it puts you instantly ahead of the pack. He thinks you're charming, worldly, smart and that you know something about the world of men!

Week 2: Find an exercise or sport that challenges you physically and mentally

For me, that was running. Each day I would run as far and as fast as I could. I put on powerful music that inspired me and when I couldn't go on any more I would tell myself that the faster I ran, the stronger I would become. And the stronger I would become, the less shit I would take from men. Because here's the thing—men are going to dish out shit to anyone they think will take it. It gives some of them great pleasure to do so. And they know their prey well when they see it so there's no escaping it. But . . . if you start to build walls around yourself by becoming stronger and stronger, you will start to notice that men who give you shit are no longer going to be a part of your life. And the ones who are kind, generous, beautiful and warm will be flocking to be part of your world. As I ran up steep hills, I'd push myself up them and I would tell myself: 'You are a strong, independent woman.' Each day I felt myself getting physically stronger and stronger, which in turn helped me become mentally stronger too.

Other things you can do to physically make you stronger:

- Boxing
- Playing tennis

- Doing weights
- Pole dancing.

The list goes on. The key is to do it *every single day* without fail. The first thing you do in the morning is your strong woman exercise.

Week 3: Getting back in the game

You are now ready to start preparing to meet men again. This means you actually do need to brush up on some of your dating skills and the rules involved when it comes to conversing with men, understanding how they tick, why sex is the defining moment when it comes to whether you'll be considered a Catch or a Toss, and so on. Reading the next few chapters in this book will help you tremendously with this process, as will this conversation I had with author of *The MANual,* Steve Santagati, and the dialogue I opened up about this with the men who read my column.[4]

Sam: What is the biggest mistake women make when it comes to finding a man after they haven't dated in a while?

Steve: Well, women don't put in the right effort. The place where so many women go wrong is that they have no idea about things men actually like.

Sam: Like what? Sex? Light banter? Humour? Fast cars?

Steve: Surprisingly, the answer is *not* sex. After you sleep with us, we want to know: 'What else have you got to offer?' Do you know anything about sports, about fishing, about the books we read, about finance, about anything? Do you know how to cook?

After I had this conversation with Steve, I asked my *Ask Sam* readers what men wished women knew or participated in, and the debate was fast and furious. But generally men agreed with Steve—women don't take an interest in their interests.

So here are the top complaints men have about women who know nothing about their worlds. And during your boot camp is the perfect time for you to get on top of all these things.

'They don't know how to drive'

While this is a huge cliché, the truth is men think that about us whether we are good drivers or not. So, during your boot camp, I want you to go for a sports car or dirt bike driving lesson. There is nothing more appealing to a man than a woman who knows what she's doing behind the wheel. And you're not only doing all these activities to keep a man's interest, you're expanding yourself and injecting a little bit of spunk and sex appeal into yourself—just in case he enters into your life quicker than you envisioned.

'Ditch the salad'

'Men love meat,' says Steve. And according to a *New York Times* article, if a woman orders the steak on a first date, she instantly gets an invitation for a second.

'It's a turn-on because it shows us that a woman understands something about our world,' says Steve. 'We're meat eaters and, if she eats meat too, it shows us that she's not completely [detached from] what's going on.'

Lana Vidler, the author of *Meals Men Love: How to Catch a Man in 3 Courses*, says a well-fed man is a happy man.[5] And as long as it has red meat in it, you're halfway there. She told me via email: 'From my research, the average Australian male likes his red meat and potatoes with chocolate mousse for dessert. Chicken schnitzel and lemon tart are a very close second.'

Oh, and ladies, it's not that hard either. The good news is that *Meals Men Love* was actually written with the career woman in mind, so now you've got no excuse to get back into the kitchen.

During your boot camp, I want you to learn at least one meat recipe. My favourite is from *Meals Men Love* and it's so simple that anyone can do it. With the author's permission, here's the recipe:

The Lamb Roast

1kg leg of lamb
2 tablespoons Worcestershire sauce
400g can cream of mushroom soup
Slit lamb, rub in sauce and soup and pop in the oven at 200°C for 90 minutes.
How easy is that!

From the Male Room

'A very wise comment that a mate's dad made was that if a girl can't cook a lamb roast, she ain't girlfriend material. Although I don't totally agree, if you can cook and she can't, problem solved as long as she makes up for it in other ways.'—**Jack**

While most women might be happy with a salad as a meal, for the blokes—not so much. The famous saying goes that the way to a man's heart is through his stomach, and this mantra might just be right. Through my interviews with men, it seems if you're a good cook, you've captured him for life.

Week 4: Swan around at all times and change the way you dress

Practise swanning around every time you step out of the house. Swanning was a new way I adopted to move around. Instead of walking with my head bowed and concentrating on my purpose of getting from A to B, I changed my thought pattern. I believed that at any moment 'the one' could be just around the corner. And I wanted to project the presence and aura of someone he would want to get to know, not just fuck. There's a difference.

#32. IF YOU WANT TO BE A GIRLFRIEND, DRESS THE PART

Practise looking like a girlfriend. If you don't know what that means, take a trip to your local shopping centre. Sit down and observe. Look carefully around you at the women who are in couples or married. You will notice that they dress differently to single women. They wear demure colours and outfits. They are often in flat shoes, jeans, a casual T-shirt or a jumper. They always look well groomed and happy. Here's a task for you: dress like this when no-one is watching or when you're just taking a trip to the supermarket. Fake it till you make it. Women who dress like a girlfriend or wife often soon become one. This is because this way of dressing attracts a different type of man—a man who actually wants to commit and have a girlfriend, rather than a player looking for some fun.

From the Male Room

'I think among women these days there is definitely the lost art of grace. Men respond well to graceful women. We look at the way you walk, hold your head, enter a room and smile. It could be anywhere from the gym to the club—but grace is so rare these

days that it's an amazing thing to finally see a woman
who actually has some. That is what I would call The
Catch.'—**Dean**

The Catch doesn't dress for sex. The desperate, weak girl does. She moves around with sex on her mind. Her cleavage is on full display. Her hair is bouncing down by her waist. She is swinging her hips. You know the type. In fact you probably hate her. You probably wish you could be her and turn every male head. You probably think that you want to be the one that every guy sees and instantly wants to fuck. But guess what? This sexual girl can't get a boyfriend. Really. She can't. It's a sad state of affairs when the sexual girl does indeed meet a guy who she semi-likes, only to suddenly realise that because of her Sex Item persona, he only wants to have his way with her. And then be gone. Because men don't want to marry the sexual girl. They want to marry the strong woman.

The outcome

Remember, a man isn't someone who is going to fill the gaps. He is potentially the icing on the cake. A cake which is rich and moist and crammed with the most delicious filling of strawberries and cream. He wants to top off the cake that is your life and have your heart, mind, body and spirit—but your cake is already brimming with goodies without him. You are so fulfilled and happy that he is constantly on his toes trying to impress you. He cannot be part of your cake until he has proven he is worthy to go anywhere near it. Seriously. Get a life before you get a man. The man you eventually get will be so much better that you'll know it was all worth it at the end.

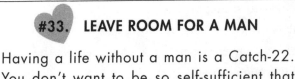

#33. LEAVE ROOM FOR A MAN

Having a life without a man is a Catch-22. You don't want to be so self-sufficient that there is no room in your life for a guy, but at the same time you don't want to be in a place whereby you are miserable without one by your side. The happy medium is being able to enjoy a balance of hanging out with your friends, being cultural, interesting and maintaining your hobbies, while still having the time and energy to be feminine, go out on dates and give a man the chance when he comes along.

If you find yourself slipping back into your old habits, delete any tempting numbers from your phone. Don't text guys with funny little thoughts or photos of yourself posing in the mirror sans your underwear. Don't tell them you're thinking of them or ask them what they're up to at 10 pm because you're bored. Get a life. Read a book. Watch TV. Call a girlfriend.

Other tips for becoming a strong woman:

- Be able to live on your own.
- Realise that it's OK to be single.
- Make new friends with random people.
- Talk to strangers.
- Go shopping for furniture.
- Get yourself a couple of wing people: they can be women or men.
- Get yourself a platonic male companion.

And remember, once you have the man of your dreams, don't think that everything stops there—or that you can start whining to him or texting him all the time or complaining to him that he's not attentive enough. Keep your cake full and brimming. Keep your friends. Keep your life. Keep reading your books and doing your exercise. Keep up your strength and continue to build on it. Of course, there is nothing better than satiating sex and romantic dates and scrumptious breakfasts for two the following morning—but remember that you've been enjoying your life by yourself, or with your girlfriends, and that you had a life before him and that you'll still continue to have a life now that he's in it—lucky him! He'll want to be in it forever if you continue to build on it.

8

How to find a man

Keeping score: How to work out what you *don't* want

Before we work out what you want in a partner, let's talk about what you don't want: a toxic man. *Sigh.* When you find yourself ensconced in the dating game, no matter what age or life stage you're at, you're bound to come across one or more of these types of men.

You know him all too well. He's the one who takes off his wedding ring at the bar, or the one who tries to get you into bed on the first date, or the worst type of all—the one who promises you the world, makes you fall in love with him (usually thanks to his fast wit, sexy looks and irresistible charm), and then vanishes into thin air before you can say, 'But I thought you loved me!'

Kanye West wrote an ode to these toxic blokes, telling the women to have a toast for their douchebags, arseholes and scumbags, and that the plan for women is to run away as fast as they can.

Which is all very well for West to advise. Run away. Yes, it would seem like the obvious thing to do, wouldn't it? But when you're engrossed in the heady drama of it all with one of these types, somehow it's not that easy.

But I thought he liked me!

But I thought he was 'the one'!

But he was sooo freaking perfect! What the hell happened?

Why women fall for the toxic man (despite his drawbacks and foibles) is obvious: he's charming, sexy and knows all the right moves. And you're not yet in the proper Catch headspace. Which means that all this drama, the ups, downs and uncertainty, is actually appealing to you. Don't worry, it won't be for much longer.

Over the past year I have dated my fair share of jerks, douchebags, arseholes and men who quite simply weren't good enough for me. Of course at the time I never saw any of the warning signs. It wasn't because I wasn't aware of the fact that the man in question didn't make me feel good—it was because I would put the blame for his behaviour on myself. Instead of walking away and telling myself I was The Catch and therefore would not accept such treatment from a man,

I kept thinking that if I did something differently or changed something about myself or the way I looked, that he would change too. No such luck. Hence in this chapter I offer you the warning signs of how to spot the man who isn't good enough for you. Because depending on where you are in this program, you may not be strong enough yet to realise this on your own.

Types of men you'll attract (and fall for) when you're not yet The Catch

The Player

You meet him, there's instant chemistry and he pushes all your buttons. You fall instantly in love with him and he woos you in all the right ways. Forget it. This man is a skilled player who knows exactly how to manipulate the game. The telltale signs he's a player is when he suddenly goes missing for a few days. Even when he calls you after being MIA and is super charming and ever the doting date, you need to fully believe that he is not busy, didn't lose your number or isn't out with his mum. Instead, you need to think (know) he's fucking someone else. Seriously. You are simply in rotation.

The Catch never accepts being part of a man's sexual rotation. The next time he calls she simply tells him she's busy and moves on with her life. She doesn't have time for players because in the end the player always wins. He just knows the game too well. And once you get caught up in his lecherous web, there is no cutting loose until your heart gets broken into a million pieces.

The player I was dating was the *worst* sort of player. He was the type who made a woman fall in love with him through his charm and charisma. He took me on the best dates possible, made all the right moves, even delayed sex! Boy, did I think I had hit the jackpot. Even when the phone calls became sporadic, and when I couldn't get hold of him whenever I tried to call him back, I didn't think something was up. In fact, it only made me like him more! Then, after two months of dating, he proceeded to tell me that he actually had a girlfriend . . . of *two years*! I couldn't believe what I was hearing! I had fantasy jumped—where you concoct an entire relationship future in your head and envision how far things might progress only to realise (later on) that the person in question was envisioning nothing of the sort. And yet the entire time, I was simply a pawn in his dating game.

Now I can spot these types from a mile away. The minute a woman asks me why a man is only calling her every five days, or only on weekends, I instantly know his game. And the women always discover that I am correct in the end. So to avoid the mistake of getting heartbroken by one of these men, get strong, know your worth and believe you're The Catch. Because

Catches don't accept scraps from men, no matter how good-looking, charming, sexy or good in bed they are.

Signs he's a Player:

- He loves the game and the strategy around picking up women.
- He pushes for sex quickly (but pretends to be nonchalant about it).
- He takes all the women he dates to the same restaurant (and tells you!).
- He tells you what you want to hear.
- He will be dating and juggling many women at once.
- He has no real and genuine desire to share a future with you.
- He will call a few times a week but inconsistently.
- He will see you on Saturday and another girl on Sunday.
- He will reel you in by making you feel good about yourself and showing you a fun time but will then pull back, which keeps you asking questions as to why it all doesn't add up.
- He seems genuine when you're together but is distant when you're apart.
- He doesn't 'man up' at the end of the day.
- He uses women, tends to be a cheater and only shows his true colours once you're hooked . . . because that's his aim!

The Jerk

When you meet a man with attitude who oozes confidence and isn't afraid to unabashedly approach you, know that this is because he is unafraid to approach any woman at any time. Even while he is dating you. Jerks make a move. Nice guys sit back and wait for some sort of signal telling them to make a move. Jerks don't try to 'befriend' women, thus never ending up in the 'friend zone'. They make their move quickly and stealthily. But here's the telltale sign you're dating a Jerk: jerks will never make a woman feel safe or secure. That's all part of his game—to keep you on edge and make you question where he is, what he's doing and then beg for him to like you. Which should be the number-one reason smart women will stay away from them.

Signs he's a Jerk:

- He's only interested in himself and never asks about you.
- He woos you one minute and forgets about you the next.
- He only contacts you when it's convenient for him.
- He thinks its strange you're questioning his lack of contact.
- Unlike the Player, he doesn't actually really care about the outcome with you, only about satisfying himself.

- He is confused about what he wants and so he acts like a Jerk in order to ensure you don't get attached.
- No amount of whining or crying will snap the Jerk out of it.

The Womaniser

Ah, the Womaniser. This dude loves women. In fact he is so in love with women that he doesn't believe that he should have just one. Hence while he shows you all the love and affection you could ever ask for, at the same time he is doing the same thing to a bevy of other unsuspecting women. You might not find out for quite some time that the Mr Perfect you're dating is actually a Womaniser in disguise as he thinks what he is doing is perfectly legitimate. Watch very carefully for red flags and flaws in his stories about his whereabouts.

Signs he's a Womaniser:
- He tells women what they want to hear regardless of what he actually means.
- He promises you the world (despite the fact he may not have a cent to his name).
- He loves wining and dining women.
- He needs a woman around to boost his ego even if he's not interested in her.
- He doesn't necessarily go in for the kill right away so as to make women think he's really the nice guy.

- He needs to be constantly reminded that he is loved and admired by women.
- He is sleazy.

The Emotional or Physical Abuser

Patricia found herself stuck in a relationship in which her partner constantly put her down. He told her she wasn't good enough for him, that she was useless around the house and that she wasn't good enough at her job. The more he put her down, the more reliant on him she became. Because that's what emotional abusers do: they squash their partners into the ground so that their self-worth becomes so low, they feel they have no choice but to stay in the unhappy relationship. It's a sad state of affairs when this occurs, because the woman gets so down on herself that she begins to blame herself for everything that goes wrong, and truly starts to believe the evil words her man dishes out to her. At the very first signs of any emotional abuse from a man, it's important that you run far, far away. Think about the fact that you will have to spend the rest of your life copping this abuse, which to me is just as bad as physical abuse. By the way, this should never ever be tolerated either.

Signs he's an Emotional or Physical Abuser:

- He is constantly putting you down with insults.
- He apologises soon after and says he'll never do it again.
- He does it again and again.

The Stringer

There's something uniquely heart wrenching about being with a stringer.

After being in an eight-year relationship, I couldn't understand why we weren't taking the next steps towards commitment. My boyfriend and I never discussed the future, and when we did it was always vague and there were never any definitive conclusions.

Deep down, I probably knew that he wasn't 'the one', or at least I wasn't the one for him, but after almost a decade together, I guess I had just assumed that one day we'd make the leap and vow to be together in sickness and in health.

What went wrong? Two years before, we'd agreed to get an apartment together. I thought I went above and beyond in playing the role of good girlfriend—I even poured the beers when the boys came over for Friday night footy. Hadn't I proved I'd be the perfect wife?

But perhaps that was the problem. I simply thought the decision was in his hands and that he'd do something about it when he was ready. No such luck.

After we called it quits, I picked up from my bookshelf a book that had long been staring back at me. Titled *Why Men Marry Some Women and Not Others* by Dr John T. Molloy, the book is a summary of a scientific study carried out by the author in an attempt to discover the differences between those couples walking out of the registry office and those walking out on each other.[6]

Molloy cites myriad reasons why some people never get married, such as not hanging out with other singles, not making the effort to go out to singles' events or go online dating, not dressing enough like a 'wife' and expecting bachelor-for-life types to morph miraculously into doting hubbies. He also says a lot of it has to do with the type of men women date. One of the most dangerous? The Stringer.

Molloy defines a Stringer as a man who loves to have a woman around to eat with, sleep with and share his life with, but, while he likes having her around full time, he never has any intention of truly committing to her.

The problem with dating a Stringer is that many of us dismiss the fact that he might be a Stringer until it's too darn late. By then, we're already heartbroken, jaded and back in the singles' world with a wall of fear around us so thick no guy could ever get through.

Molloy's tactic for dealing with stringers before it's too late? Give yourself a six-month deadline. 'If he doesn't commit to you within six months, get rid of him.'

You are also to pay no attention to his excuses nor when he tells you 'it's too soon to discuss', that he doesn't know whether or not he likes you or he hasn't decided what he feels about you.

'He is likely to tell you anything that will get you to stick around without his needing to make a commitment. Don't fall for it. The chances a Stringer will marry are very slim; he is simply not the marrying kind.'

Signs he's a Stringer:

- He never mentions commitment.
- He never mentions marriage, or recoils when you do.
- He says he wants to be single forever.
- He is selfish with his time.
- He doesn't make you a priority.
- He doesn't see relationships as a priority.
- You have been going out with him for more than enough time and still there is no sign of commitment.

A WORD ON SEX, LIES AND WHO THE CATCH SHOULD WATCH OUT FOR

Here's a word of warning: despite the fact that you make a man wait and you ensure that you don't rush the act of jumping into bed with him, it still doesn't mean that he is into you, likes you or will commit to you.

The Manipulator

There's a man I know; let's call him the Manipulator. Over the years he's learned that, to get what he wants—regular sex from a woman—he has to form some sort of a 'relationship'. And so he fakes one. Or two. Or five. All at once. He manipulates women into thinking that he is the perfect man by wining, dining and treating them with the perfect blend of chivalry and bad-boy-turned-good persona.

'I've changed,' he purrs lovingly to each and every one of them. 'And you've been the one to change me.' Cue female hearts melting, skirts lifting and—before too long—hearts breaking.

The Manipulator doesn't rush these women. Oh no. He moves slowly and stealthily, knowing very well that slow and steady wins the race. Or at least another blow job.

'Wow, he's waited so long!' the unsuspecting women say, clapping their hands in glee, imagining themselves walking down the aisle and what their babies might look like.

'He must really like me!' Or worst of all: 'I think I might have finally found "the one"!' And so they succumb to sleeping with him. And he laughs smugly to himself when another one bites the dust . . .

There are thousands of Manipulators trawling nightclubs and bars, searching for unsuspecting female victims on the hunt for a boyfriend, a husband or a part-time ATM. A Manipulator can spot their prey instantly, knows just how to dupe them and then how to toss them aside like a used piece of gum once he's gotten what he wanted out of them.

Signs he's a Manipulator:
- He tells you everything you want to hear.
- He rushes intimacy.

- He drops the bomb—after you're in love with him—that he never really wanted a girlfriend but thinks you're 'fun' to hang out with.
- He plays mind games with you.
- You always feel on edge when you don't hear from him.

The Career Bachelor

The Career Bachelor has a thriving career. He works fourteen-hour days, makes a tonne of money and thrives on his ability to make deals, make even more cash and spend it to his heart's content. But he knows that his lavish lifestyle and ability to push himself hard aren't going to last forever. And so he's made an executive decision not to let anything—or anyone—stand in his way. Including a woman. Yet since he has all the tools in the world available to him to wine and dine any woman, and have them fall hopelessly in love at his feet, he still wants to use them to his best advantage . . . for as long as he can get away with it without having to make any sort of formal commitment.

A Career Bachelor is a little more difficult to spot, navigate, deal with and get over. He will wine and dine you, romance you and woo you until the point when he discovers that you need a little more attention than he has time to give you. Once that takes place, he quickly brushes you off—too late to avoid heartbreak if you're already in love with him, which is tough not to do with men like the Career Bachelor considering they have all the perks and give you all the reasons to fantasy jump to imagining your future together. But as one such guy recently told me: 'I like having a girl in my life, up until the point where she demands more of me than I want to give at the moment. I'm avoiding commitment at all costs so that I can focus on my job. Getting a proper girlfriend means I won't be able to give her or the relationship the respect it deserves—or at least that's what I tell her in the hope it will soften the blow.'

Signs he's a Career Bachelor:

- He is obsessed with his work.
- His work always comes first.
- He works extremely long hours.
- Rather than see you, he prefers to laze around on the weekends because he is so tired from work.
- He's had a series of quick, fruitless relationships that go nowhere but just fill his spare time.
- He complains about having to take you on dates when he could be working or sleeping, or preparing for work the next day.
- He is driven purely by money and success.

The Male Spinster

Then there's the Male Spinster. He's the over-40 single dude who doesn't exactly have any intention of settling down any time soon. And why should he? He can get any woman he wants from 20 to 40 years old and he has no desire to pick just one for the long haul. Sure, you will easily fall in love with his charm, charisma, togetherness, manliness and sexual prowess. But if you think he's going to commit any time soon, don't count your bets just yet.

George Clooney is one such type. With no signs of ever settling down (he's over 50), he once had Nicole Kidman bet him £10,000 that he would be married by 40. He's since mailed her back the cheque, saying 'Double or nothing for another ten years.' She lost again.

Signs he's a Male Spinster:
- No relationship of his has lasted more than a few months.
- He is always looking for the next challenge.
- He is constantly looking over his shoulder at other women when he is out with you.
- He thrives on attention from women.
- He seems to only like women who are out of his league/age bracket.
- He prefers to go out clubbing than have quiet nights in with you.
- He is always out with his single friends.
- He has many, many women on his speed dial.

My point? The Catch needs to be a little more aware of the fact that sometimes men want sex (and will do or say anything to get it) and women want relationships (and will do or believe anything if they think one is on the horizon). While the sexually liberated among you might throw up your hands in protest and declare that not all women want a relationship, it's actually been statistically proven.

A study carried out by James Madison University, and published in the journal *Sex Roles*, discovered that most women do want a relationship and no matter how sexually liberated they are, they still fear that casual sex will lead them to become emotionally attached to the dude they've just bonked.[7] Only a measly 2 per cent of women said they strongly preferred hooking up to a relationship, while 17 per cent of men preferred casual sex over the whole wining and dining shebang. (By my reckoning, the stat is way higher for the men!)

The reason for the stats being this way is in the biological make-up of the sexes. Men physically need a 'release' due to the build-up of semen in their testes, which then tells their brain that they need sexual satisfaction in order to release it . . . and fast.

Women, on the other hand, are biologically wired to be more picky about what they do with who. After all, sex is a big investment for gals because it can lead to nine months of pregnancy and eighteen years of child rearing. Combined with the fact that women's brains don't tell them they need a physical release every twenty-four to forty-eight hours, and it's obvious why a relationship is more appealing than just a one-night stand.

Of course we can always ignore stats and biology and surmise that not all men want sex—even the subsets of blokes I've spoken about above. That it's simply a case of the media, men's magazines and the sex trade giving us false impressions that macho men are incapable of love and feelings and commitment and companionship. But, as a single girl, when all you meet out and about are Players and Stringers and so on, it's tough to comprehend that there are any men who think differently. But The Catch knows all too well how to spot these guys from a mile away. Learn this manoeuvre early in the game and you'll never get burnt.

Part 3

Now You're The Catch . . . Where is *He*?

A Cautionary Tale: Amanda

'Cheers to my future wife!' J.J. said, completing his speech to his gorgeous ex-model wife-to-be Amanda at their engagement party. The who's who of the society pages had come to celebrate the joining together of this romantic twosome. Not to mention every television and magazine journalist, too, to chronicle this momentous social occasion.

Amanda stood quietly in the corner, not daring to utter a word, a fake smile plastered on her face. J.J. had been blowing up a lot lately, and she was determined not to let anything ruin her special day, including his mood swings. In fact, ever since they'd become engaged, she felt like she was constantly tiptoeing on eggshells around him, and that he was constantly looking for ways to put her down. She looked across the crowd and tried to give them her best winning smile. Dressed in a sparkly silver minidress that shimmered as she walked, with killer stilettos she'd bought straight from the Jimmy Choo catalogue, Amanda was the epitome of elegance. She truly shone. A pity J.J. didn't seem to notice. Sure, for the cameras and the crowds he hammed it up. But lately, it seemed to Amanda that her only purpose was to be his handbag in front of the cameras. The kind, doting fiancé she saw tonight was definitely not the man she was going to face when they got home . . .

'*Honey!*' *He was gesturing for her to come over and pointing to a woman with a curly mop of dull brown hair and reading glasses perched on her nose.*

'OK! Magazine *want to take a photo and get a few quotes from you.*' *As she came closer he gripped her wrist and then put his arm around her waist.*

'*Say cheese!*'

A Cautionary Tale: Camilla

Camilla arrived at Amanda's engagement party sans date. She looked around and noticed that every person there was coupled-up. Every. Single. Person. What the fuck is wrong with me? *she thought. She was attractive, didn't have an addiction, was smart, warm, friendly and kind.*

'Why the hell don't I have a boyfriend?' she whispered sadly to Kate, who was standing there smiling like a schoolgirl next to Joey, who looked dashing in a black suit and silver tie.

'Because this is your time to get to know yourself,' Kate told her, pulling her aside. 'You had a boyfriend when we all didn't. He wasn't right for you. And you won't find someone right until you get to know every aspect of yourself without a man by your side.'

'So then why is this so bloody painful?'

Camilla looked at Amanda and J.J. She knew they had problems, but at least Amanda was engaged. At least Amanda had a man by her side. What the hell was wrong with Camilla? She had no idea. All she knew was that she had to fix it—and fast. She glanced down at her phone to see if there were any text messages from any of the men she'd kind of been seeing. Nothing. She sighed, got into a cab and went home. She needed a plan; one that would work, now. Camilla Mason was not a single, desperate girl. She was not. *So when the fuck had she become one? Well, it was time to change. Time to step up her game. Time to turn the tables.*

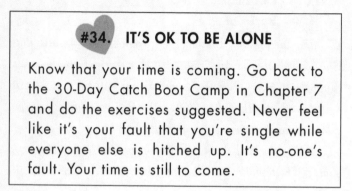

#34. IT'S OK TO BE ALONE

Know that your time is coming. Go back to the 30-Day Catch Boot Camp in Chapter 7 and do the exercises suggested. Never feel like it's your fault that you're single while everyone else is hitched up. It's no-one's fault. Your time is still to come.

A Cautionary Tale: Meg

Meg was dancing up a storm in the middle of the dance floor. This no-sex thing isn't so bad, she thought to herself. She finally had time for her friends, she'd lost weight and she looked smashing in a bright red, strapless minidress. She wasn't even searching the room for a man to fuck. She was actually just enjoying herself with her friends. She couldn't remember the last time she felt this free, this alive, this confident.

A man tapped her on the shoulder. 'Excuse me, but your tag is hanging out the back of your dress.'

'Oh yeah? So what?' she replied, and continued to dance.

'I like your attitude,' he said.

She noticed he had an accent. 'You American?' she asked.

'Canadian,' he said. 'No biggie. Everyone gets it wrong. I'm a distant cousin of J.J. Decided to make the trip for the engagement. Didn't want to give up a chance to get to Australia.'

Meg looked him up and down. Definitely not her usual style—he was casually dressed, and had an innocence in his eyes that she didn't usually notice in the men who approached her. Usually they looked hungry, and stared at her like a piece of meat that they wanted to devour.

'Friend of the bride?' he asked her.

'Yeah. My best friend.'

'What's your name?'

'Meg,' she said, extending a well-manicured hand.

'Hey, I'm Mark.'

Meg and Mark. Interesting. He began to dance beside her. She noticed he was kind of goofy, and she began to giggle. He grinned back at her.

'Want to go outside for a drink?'

'What!' she yelled above the music.

'Want to go outside for a drink?' he yelled into her ear.

She could have sworn she heard 'kink' instead, but she brushed that thought from her mind.

'Sure, whatever.'

He grabbed two glasses of champagne off a tray from a nearby waiter, took her hand and led her outside.

'So, Meg, the most beautiful girl in the room,' he said, looking at her incredulously, 'I want to hear all about yourself . . .'

 #35. THE DATING HIATUS WILL COME TO AN END

You'll know exactly the moment the hiatus will come to an end. It happens naturally— you start to feel a sense of freedom, independence and peacefulness that you haven't felt before. Then it's time . . . and he—your dream man—will bounce right into your life.

Cautionary Tales: Meg and Kate

When Meg met Mark, something inside her snapped. The night of the engagement party the two of them stayed up talking for hours and hours. Meg was intrigued by this confident man who didn't seem to have only one thing on his mind at all. He was intelligent, cool and had even graduated top of his class at Stanford. Now this is a Catch, *she thought to herself.* Maybe I should seduce him? *No, no, no. She knew the moment she began her sexual hiatus that things were going to be different. And she was determined to prove to everyone that she really could change. That she really could start to open herself up to something true, honest and real.*

After she met Mark, she began to clean out her sex-saturated life. She began by deleting every man she had on speed dial, every guy who called her for booty calls. Then she threw out all her crotchless underwear, her different-sized condoms, her whips and chains and garter belts. She vowed she was really going to give Mark the chance he deserved. And she couldn't have any distractions.

Meanwhile, Kate had summoned Camilla to another emergency meeting.

'Camilla, we have a problem,' Kate said, downing her espresso martini and stabbing at a prawn with her fork. 'I think I'm in love with Joey.'

'Wow, that's amazing! What's so bad about that?'

'What do you mean?' Kate snapped back. 'He's supposed to be a party boy! Something for fun! We're supposed to just be having fun together! I can't love him! It's not right!'

Camilla sighed. Joey was adorable. He was everything any girl would want in a man. Except, of course, for the fact that he was way, way too young. But she knew that Kate had finally allowed herself to fall for him.

'Plus, think about this: he's so young that when I'm, like, 40, he'll still be in his twenties! I'll be the old hag running after my playboy boyfriend. And what about when he has all these beautiful 20-year-olds running after him, then what? What am I supposed to do? And I want to get married soon . . . I can't make a 24-year-old propose!'

'I'll stop you right there. If Demi Moore can do it with saggy knees and a flat chest, you can do it.'

Kate sighed. 'Can you believe how much I've changed since that trip to Miami?'

Camilla couldn't, but Kate had done it. She'd seriously rid herself of her bad-boy addiction and she'd come out the other side with her perfect man in her arms. The funny thing was, Camilla thought, that Joey was nothing Kate had previously had on her lengthy checklist. He was the wrong age, had the wrong profession, lived in the wrong part of town—but Kate didn't seem to care. Which made Camilla think that sometimes The Catch isn't always who he seems . . .

And then Joey arrived. He gave Kate a big kiss on the lips. He paid for the girls' drinks. And then he took Kate home.

Camilla walked back to her apartment alone. She was ecstatic for Kate. Joey wasn't the kind of man she herself was after. But who was? Surely if even Kate could find a normal relationship, she could?

9

Meeting him

Talking to him

Opening lines and the art of the female pick-up: What
to say, how to say it and how to ensure he thinks that
talking to you was all his brilliant idea.

This chapter might sound contrary to everything
you've learned in the previous chapters. But let me start
by saying that this isn't a section on how to ask out a
man who you've secretly been lusting after your entire
life. Instead, this is a chapter about how to practise
talking to men, and getting them to ask *you* out, so that
when the real 'one' comes along, you are filled with
confidence and have the know-how to speak to him,
understand his reactions to certain things and know
more about what he responds to well, and what he

won't respond to at all. After all, practice makes perfect. So let's get to it!

From the Male Room

> *'I like to go to either the local bar where I can watch some sports (AFL, NRL, etc.) and I could be anywhere around the city. I think sporting events are great to meet nice women, and the airport too! I prefer bars where the atmosphere is good and it is not like a meat market.'*—**Trent**

> *'If you want to know where I hang out, try responding to my profile on RSVP!'*—**Mick**

How to pick up men

Don't laugh. Men do it in droves. They pick up (or at least attempt to strike up conversations with women) in coffee shops, at the gym, on the train and in nightclubs. They talk to women using lines and pick-up tactics, and often without an agenda other than to have a little fun, get a little practice and then go onto the next. And what ends up happening? Sometimes they get ignored, sometimes they get laughed at, sometimes they get a number, and sometimes they even score a date! But either way, the more they practise, the better they get at it. So that when a woman they're really interested in comes along, they know exactly what works and what doesn't. They know what to say to push the right female buttons and they're so used to rejection that it doesn't really matter about the outcome. They simply put their best (practised) foot forward and cross their fingers and hope for the best.

So, why not flip the whole thing on its head? Why shouldn't women have the skills and the know-how to do the same? Why shouldn't women quit thinking ahead a couple of years to the aisle, the ring and the white dress, and concentrate on the *now*?

Of course the notion of 'picking up' has long been the domain of men. After all, it's in their DNA to want to hunt, capture and then have their way with their prey. Hence they've spent centuries learning the ways to capture a woman's heart—as fast and hard as possible. From Casanova and his lair where he enticed women with satiating hot chocolate, to the modern-day pick-up artists and the likes of players like Charlie Sheen, men have it down to a fine science.

Women have always been the more subtle creatures, waiting in the wings while preening and primping themselves in order to attract the most appealing male's attention.

And who's happier? The men, of course.

The truth is that men don't cry or go into deep despair when a one-night fling doesn't turn into a full-blown, long-term relationship. They simply pick themselves up and move onto the next, all the while rehearsing and finessing their pick-up artistry skills so that they are able to talk to women anywhere, anytime.

What if I told you that you could pick up men in a way that would make them believe they did all the hard work? What if I told you that you could actually say certain lines to the men you meet in order to make them actually want to chase you? What if I told you that the better you learned how to talk to men first, the more chance you had at becoming The Catch, and that better opportunities would become available to you?

'But why should women have to pick up men?' you might be wondering. 'Shouldn't men do all the chasing and women just sit back and wait for them to do all the hard work?'

Well, yes. But the trouble these days is that modern men have become shit-scared of rejection. We've ruined the blokes with all our games, rules and regulations, and now none of them will dare approach women and be straightforward about their intentions. Ever.

The biggest obstacle modern women face is not whether Mr Right really exists (he does and he's looking for you right now). Or how to keep him interested for more than a nanosecond (don't return his calls, make him chase and don't sleep with him too soon). Or even how to tell whether or not he'll be good in bed (check out the size of his hands, the way he dances and how well he kisses).

Instead the biggest obstacle modern women now face is simply this: *Where the bloody hell is he?* And when you do find the poor sod, how in the world do you get him to ask you out on a date without coming across like a desperate floozy with an 'I-want-to-get-married-now!' sticker plastered on your forehead?

You play it like a man. And then you win it like a woman . . . and get him to catch you.

Sam's Catch adventures

In order to test out my theories, I agreed to meet public relations manager Courtney for breakfast and some serious female pick-up training. Her fiery red hair, pin-up-girl lips and curves to rival Dita Von Teese were the first things I noticed as I sat down and we ordered frappes. She wanted to know why not one man had spoken to her the night before at a club, let alone asked for her number.

'I haven't been asked out on a date in months,' she told me sadly. 'I'm ready for a boyfriend. Where is he?'

I asked her where she stood in the bar, what kind of expression she had on her face and what she was wearing.

'I don't know, I haven't really thought about it. I'm just so annoyed at the whole situation that I probably don't have a very nice expression on my face,' she replied.

Then I told her that her first mistake was that she was wearing a giant 'fuck off' sticker on her forehead.

'Well I was standing alone, what was I supposed to do? Just start smiling at strangers?'

Yes! I told her to soften up, to smile and to understand the first thing about men: they're shit-scared of rejection. I told her that all women need to do is smile and say hi. She didn't believe me.

♥ #36.   GET A MAN TO ASK YOU OUT

The way to do this is quite simple: smile, nod your head in their direction when they look back at you, hold their gaze for three seconds, and then say something— anything—and they'll be elated that you actually spoke to them. If you zip it shortly after that and let them do the rest, they'll be none the wiser about your pick-up skills.

'So then what? They'll just come over and talk to you if you do that?' Courtney asked.

Well, sometimes. I explained to her that if that doesn't work, there's a series of lines that women can use to engage men in conversation. She responded by telling me that the very thought of using 'lines' was way too desperate and that she'd never ever contemplate doing it.

'They'll know,' she said, shaking her head. 'I'm not that type of girl.'

I've heard my theory being shut down all too often. But ever since the Big Fucking Break-up, I've tried and tested it. And I've proved it works. I decided to demonstrate. I told her that there's hope for single girls like us, and I said it really loudly. The man at the table adjacent to ours smiled to himself. I knew he was listening. I knew I had a three-second window. And so I pounced.

❤ #37. GET A MAN'S ATTENTION QUICKLY AND THEN SAY SOMETHING

If you notice a man staring at you or looking in your direction, you have a three-second window within which to say something to him—otherwise it can come across creepy and unnatural. Just pick any topic—ask what he's drinking, notice something he's wearing, ask him a question about the place you're at— *anything*! Ask one or two follow-up questions and then zip it. Let him do the rest!

'It's hard for single girls out there, don't you think?' I said to him, smiling. 'I mean, aren't all guys really scared of rejection so they won't ask us out in the first place?'

'Well, they're pretty stupid then, 'cause you girls are gorgeous,' the man replied. He leaned in and we got a better look. He had salt-and-pepper hair and his skin was tanned and slightly lined. His eyes were piercingly blue. He asked Courtney about her dreams (yes, he launched right into it!) and she told him she wanted to sail around the world on a yacht. He told us he's a sailor and was about to embark on such a voyage. They exchanged numbers and then he finished his breakfast and told her he'd call her.

Suddenly there was a fresh sparkle in her eye. A light had gone on in her head.

'Wow. That wasn't desperate at all. Did we even do anything?'

Indeed we did. We smiled, engaged in a conversation and then let him do the work.

Afterwards she told me that she'd usually have just ignored men like him. Or scoffed and baulked if he'd dared to even talk to her. I told her that the last thing on his mind was the fact that we picked him up and, even if she wasn't interested in him, it was all just for practice anyway.

The other thing I love about doing this is that she will walk around for the rest of the day with her head held high, smiling at everyone and basking in the knowledge that a cute guy asked for her number earlier that day. The men who spot her during the day will sense her energy, and will instantly think of her as a Catch. I don't even need to tell you why. Just read Chapter 12, the male reaction to the Catch strategy, about what exactly goes on when he senses there's competition around.

We left breakfast and Courtney was elated. There was a new bounce in her step. She was smiling at everyone. As we walked down the street towards her car, two men passed by and said hi to her.

'Wow, I smile and the world smiles back at me,' she said in a dreamy voice. I smiled back at her. Then I explained to her how the process works when you actually meet a man you like.

The art of the female pick-up

- Stand in an open, available place in the room.
- Wear less make-up and have soft hair.
- Smile.
- Speak to a man first about something that you notice about him or mention something that is happening around you. You can also ask him for a male opinion on something. Lines to use:
  - ★ What are you drinking?
  - ★ How good is the DJ?
  - ★ Does it get busier in here?
  - ★ Can you give me your opinion on something? My friend just went on a date with a guy the other night and he didn't pay. So she had to foot the whole bill! Do you think that's wrong?
  - ★ Do you think women should be able to ask out men?
- Once you've attempted your pick-up, zip it and let him do the rest.
- After you've engaged him in a conversation and he starts trying to impress you, you can casually

let him know that you're heading out somewhere later on and that he and his mates are welcome to join. This is known in male pick-up circles as the 'bounce'.

How to get a man to get your number

So, you've met an awesome guy. You would very much like to see him again. You have to leave, or he has to leave, and you can see that he's not going to ask for your number, even though you felt some sparks flying. So how do you ensure that you carry out the great number swap? Easy.

Somewhere within your conversation he would have mentioned to you something that you might have been interested in. Make sure you take note of this and how you can get involved. So, for instance, if he says something like, 'Oh, I love sailing, I go sailing every single weekend!' Then you can say something like, 'Oh, I love sailing too! But I don't have a boat!' Or, 'I love sailing and I'd love to learn!'

Then you zip it, and wait for him to respond with something like, 'Oh great, well you should come sailing sometime!'

And then you can say, 'Oh cool, well, want to take my number then?'

The same conversation can work with anything that you might have peppered into the conversation. Don't bother taking his number. You're not going to call him. He needs to call you if he wants to see you. He's got your number. Don't think about it again.

10

A word on internet dating

Once you're The Catch, you might think that the way to meet a man is to go online. After all there are, like, one million guys out there just waiting with bated breath to meet a Catch like you!

There is nothing wrong with going online to meet a man, but you need to know a few things before you do it. Namely, that almost every man on these websites is after the same thing: to see how quickly and cheaply he can get you into bed. The good news is that there are indeed some nice guys out there who are in it to find a girlfriend, but that means you're going to have to be super smart in weeding them out. As part of my job in writing this book, I went online dating. I carefully chose a profile picture of myself that made me look super fun, cute and *not a day* younger than my actual age. You don't want a man rocking up to the date and gasping in surprise at how old you really are!

The next thing I did was to chat online to any of the men who seemed interesting or who were keen to ask me out. What I noticed instantly was this: there are certain men on these dating websites who even before speaking to you or getting to know anything about you, invite you out for a drink. These are the men I want you to stay away from. No matter how cute he looks in his online photo, I want you to have at least *two* phone conversations with the man you are interested in *before* you decide to go out for a drink with him. Also, I found that if they were asking me out that quickly, they were filling up their weekly schedule with one date after another, every single night. And that they were not in it to really get to know someone, but instead were just using it as a way to get female attention and perhaps to get them into bed.

So, after you speak to a man on the phone a few times and you decide that you really do want to meet him in person, you are within your rights to ask him for a few extra photos of himself. I always like to make sure I have at least three or four photos of this man before I commit to a date.

The location, time and place of the date is extremely important. I like to choose somewhere that is *really* close to where I live. That way I can exit swiftly if I choose. Make sure that you just say 'drinks' and make it early, so you can always have an escape route when things aren't going well. You can use the line: 'I have dinner plans with a girlfriend tonight, but thought I'd meet you for a drink first.'

Always tell a friend exactly where you are going, what time you are going, and that you will call them at a certain time during the night, and then again when you get home. If they don't hear from you, they know it's time to send out a search party!

The most important thing with online dating is to stick stringently by these rules. You don't know this person at all. He is a complete stranger to you. None of your friends know him, nor your colleagues, nor your housemate. So you need to make sure that not only do you carefully vet him, but that you put your best, most classy, foot forward.

That means *no kissing* on the first date. If you ensure that you do not kiss him (and *definitely not sleep with him*) on the first date, he will not think you are the type of girl who is kissing and sleeping with every single man you meet online. You can be honest and open about where you work and what you do, but if you think that you are not into him and that there is a chance that he might stalk you or follow you or do something crazy, just be vague with the details.

I actually ended up really liking the man I met online. He was smart, charming, good-looking, interesting and fun. He took me on a number of dates and he was quite the gentleman!

His work ended up posting him to a different city and I decided that before we let things develop any further, I was going to move on. No more internet dating for me, but this, too, was straight after my 30-Day

Man Hiatus. It helped me get back into the dating game and it served its purpose.

If anything, internet dating gives your ego a huge boost that it might need after the hiatus. With so many men trying to court you all at once, you instantly inject that feeling of confidence and invincibility into your personality, which gets noticed instantly by the man who you really want to attract! So use internet dating to your advantage—it's ripe for the picking!

A Cautionary Tale: Amanda

Things only went downhill for Amanda and J.J. God, he was a prick. What a moron! What the hell was she thinking?

At the launch of her 'Jazz it Up' swimwear label a few days after the engagement party all the cameras were on Amanda and her man as they lounged on a canary-yellow couch in a private cabana at the Ivy Pool Club, sipping on fig tree martinis. They say you haven't 'arrived' in the fashion biz unless you can score yourself a seat at one of these coveted cabanas, usually reserved for visiting Hollywood celebrities. The pool, an urban oasis set high atop an office building in the midst of the CBD with tropical palms and a cool DJ, was the place to see and be seen. Not to mention the fact you could be mistaken for thinking you were lounging at a beachside retreat in St Tropez.

And everyone was there for her too: Camilla, Kate and Meg, plus various It and society girls. She looked through her oversized YSL vintage sunglasses towards the pool and took in the glam set lounging on aqua lilos. Young girls with high cheekbones wearing Amanda's low-riding bikinis flirted with boys in tight shorts and tattoos, their Raybans perched neatly on their chiselled faces.

Amanda certainly looked like she belonged, in a flowing gold and green caftan, large gold hoop earrings and her sig-nature red hair loose, flowing and wavy. Yes, life was pretty *freaking perfect for the bikini designer. The runway show of her first range the previous night had received rave reviews, and she had her own television segment on the FTV network.*

Out of the corner of her eye, she looked at her fiancé sitting next to her and took in his bulging biceps, sun-bleached blond hair and the fact that every eye was probably more focused on them as a couple than the bikini range itself. Not that she minded. The thought of everyone lusting after what she had was what kept her going. Even though she knew deep down that it wasn't exactly as perfect as it all seemed. Yes, there was one thing niggling her about J.J. But she decided to brush it off for now. That was until someone accidentally nudged J.J.'s arm.

'Fuck!' J.J. yelled, spilling his drink onto his white shirt. 'Stupid fucker. Doesn't anyone watch where they're going? Where the fuck is the waiter?'

Camilla and Kate exchanged knowing looks, but Amanda didn't notice. Or at least she pretended not to.

'Darling,' Amanda replied calmly, gritting her teeth. 'Wait here. I'll get you some soda water.' She stood up and, towering over him, she gave him a kiss on the head.

'Are you kidding me?' he cried, jerking his head back. 'You have no fucking idea, do you? This shit stains. And it's a fucking new Prada shirt.'

Amanda bit her tongue. She had spent the last six months putting up with his moods, and knew she was going to have spend the next three hours doing the same, not to mention the rest of her life. The mere thought gave her a headache.

'I can't stay here like this. I'm going home,' J.J. snapped.

She'd grown used to his temper. She figured that it was just a by-product of being the arm candy of such a famous man. And he was extremely generous—at least most of the time. Besides, her business was flourishing and they were photographed together in the paper every single weekend, which was doing wonders for her brand recognition. So what harm could a little bad language being flung at her really do?

#38. LOOK CAREFULLY AT THE EMOTIONALLY ABUSIVE MAN . . . AND RUN

Usually he behaves the way he does because his own self-esteem is so low that he likes to pull others down along with himself. The quicker you get rid of him, the better off you'll be.

Amanda watched J.J. turn on his heel without even saying goodbye, and took in a deep breath. Camilla squeezed her hand, but she didn't want solace. In fact she didn't want anyone feeling sorry for her. She loved J.J. Heck, he was everything she'd always wanted! Surely she could put up with a few mood swings here and there?

She let the heat beat down on her face for a minute, pulled herself together and plastered her smile back on. She had bikinis to sell. And appearances to keep up. And she wasn't going to let anyone—especially not the people who looked up to her—see her cry.

11

The first three dates

The Catch on a date

Dating is supposed to be fun, right? So why is it so freaking painful? I'll tell you why: because you aren't entering into it with the right attitude. Too many women go on dates thinking about how they are going to impress a man. Newsflash: it's his duty to work out how he's going to impress *you*. That's right, all you need to do is show up. Really, it's that simple.

The Catch is a mastermind on a date. This is where she wields most of her power. Because men these days have so much choice, they use the date as an opportunity to really give you a run for your money. These days men will test women on dates. They will ask them questions, and look carefully at everything from what she eats to how often she picks up her mobile phone to what she says about her girlfriends.

I know, it's a horrible business, but men these days think they're clued in. They don't want to end up with someone who is high maintenance, not even for a second date. So here's how to pass their tests with flying colours. You might not agree with everything you're about to read, but trust me when I say if you follow these rules down to the letter, I'll guarantee you'll get a second date. But here's the rub: the real reason you're going on a date is not so you can impress the man, but so that the man can impress *you*.

Catches are not thinking, 'Am I going to be enough for him?', but rather, 'Is he going to be enough for *me*?'

And whether you like him or not, every date you go on should be practice for becoming Catch material.

The first date rules

So you've scored yourself a hot date. Bravo! But now what? Surely it can't be too hard ... right? So he called (or texted, or Facebooked) and invited you out for dinner, lunch, coffee, whatever. You think you've got everything sorted, your excitement is raging and you're looking forward to finally going on a date with a potential Mr Right. Sorry ladies, but I'm going to have to stop you right there.

Unfortunately these days, thanks to the proliferation of internet dating, speed dating and every other type of dating out there, first dates no longer get the consideration they deserve. In fact, everyone is so quick to size each other up and to ascertain in thirty minutes (if you're lucky!) whether or not you're 'the one' that first dates have become more like gruelling job interviews than something that is supposed to be the beginning phase of allowing you to get to know one another.

Because let's face it: if it doesn't work out with the first person, many are under the illusion they can simply hop online and try again with the next willing suitor! No wonder there are more singletons out there than ever before.

But if you think that the person you're about to head out on a first date with deserves more than just a quick meal and a kiss on the cheek goodbye, then listen up, because there are a bunch of sure-fire methods that will ensure you get a follow-up phone call, another date and maybe even a relationship out of it! So read on . . .

1. Your attitude

First things first. I need you to ask yourself a question: How am I going to approach this date? Most people go into it with the mindset that they have to act like the perfect person and be like some out-of-this-world creature in order to impress the person they're about to rendezvous with. So they get all nervous and end up talking too much and going off on tangents and drinking too much and basically putting themselves at a mighty disadvantage. But think about it—why go to all the trouble to impress someone on the first date when you hardly even know if they're worthy of you yet? After all it's a first bloody date—you don't even know the guy!

Think about this: if you were on a date and you didn't really know the person but they were doing everything in their power to impress you because they'd already decided in their heads how fabulous you are and what a great Catch you are and how desperately they want to be with you, would you be instantly attracted to them? Or would you think that since you have all the power, and they're a little desperate (OK, majorly desperate), you might as well play the field until you feel like it's time to call them back? Of course you would do the latter. That's how nature works. Red-blooded humans always want what they can't have, or something they feel is slightly out of their reach and therefore worthy of their attention.

So the key to going on a first date (or any encounter that you may have with a man you're not yet certain about) is that you need to change your mindset. You need to start to believe that *you* are The Catch, and that you are sizing him up on the date and have yet to make your decision. In fact if anyone needs to do the impressing, it's *him*!

Also your decision to go on a second date with him doesn't come cheaply either. You need to make him work for it. I'm not saying he needs to take you to the most expensive restaurant in the city. But he needs to earn your attention, your trust, your respect and allow you to let your feelings grow by chasing you! And if you notice that his behaviour is not congruent with the type of behaviour you know you deserve (he makes you pay, makes you wait, cancels at the last minute or talks incessantly about an ex), you can by all means politely thank him for the date and then refuse a second one when he begs for it.

Knowing your worth in this way is extremely important when it comes to attracting a man who is good enough for you and who will make you happy in the long run. Why be stuck with a dude you've settled for, when a great man could be just around the corner? It's up to you to make the decisions and to make him work for your affections. And don't be shy about making him try to impress you! Men are hunters by nature and if you really sit back and allow him to do the chasing, you'd be surprised at what you discover.

The trouble is that he won't chase overnight. But the number-one reason men have told me as to why they don't call women is simply this: she called him first! Don't be that girl. Please.

2. What you wear

Despite having the best attitude, or making sure you've done everything right in the lead-up to the date, men are still visual creatures. The guys I've polled tend to notice everything from how much make-up you wear to what you eat! So in order to make your first date experience as smooth as possible, you need to be aware of the things he notices most about you on the date.

Men judge you with their eyes. Usually within the first thirty seconds of meeting you. So if you look like a meal on a platter being served up to him—that is, showing too much leg or cleavage, wearing too much make-up or perfume—he's immediately going to put you into the 'trying too hard to impress me' category. There's no challenge left for him. It's boring. He knows he can have you with a click of his fingers. And before he's even heard what you've got to say, he's moving on to someone who he feels has a higher price and a bigger value. Because the harder things are to get, the more men want them!

From the Male Room

'A woman should wear something nice and a bit sexy. A nice pair of jeans, a nice top, jacket and high heels is always good. Or a nice dress that is not too revealing and can be comfortable too. Some girls have dressed a little too sluttily on a date and I think that can give out the wrong impression and a vibe that she is easy and she is just wanting a night out and a good time. If the woman drinks too much then that is a deal breaker too.'—**Tyrone**

So with that being said, dress like you would if you were going out on the town with your girlfriends. You're not trying to woo them—you're trying to look sexy for yourself. And here's another thing—of all the men I've interviewed, not a single one of them has ever commented on the brand name of a woman's shoes. Or the fact that he was impressed because she went out shopping that day for a new dress (which cost more than her weekly rent). Or that she got her hair specially straightened, a spray tan and a set of false eyelashes. Sure, it's important to be well groomed. In fact, I recommend that you always do your nails, wear a scented body moisturiser, have clean hair and clean clothes. But doing all that other stuff—like stressing over the brand

---

 #39. DRESS LIKE YOU MIGHT MEET HIM

There are many single women who think that they can simply wear their casual gear, hair tied back and walk around comfortably in their gym sweats sans make-up in all their spare time. But the single girl can meet a man anywhere, at any time. Standing in the grocery store, at the gym, in the library— wherever. Always have your Single Catch outfit on: a dab of lipgloss, a sexy T-shirt, cute shorts or tight jeans and a kitten heel. You just never know when you're going to bump into 'the one'.

name of your shoes—doesn't really matter to men. (In fact, if you skip the fake eyelashes, too much tan and the false nails, they'll like you more!)

Here's what men have told me: they like women who look hot. Period. So if looking hot means you get to pull out one of your favourite trusted LBDs and a cute pair of heels or ankle boots you've had for a while, don't stress that you're not dressed to the nines in the latest Jimmy Choos or Alexander Wang ensemble. Men don't notice brands. They notice the way you wear your clothes or the swaying of your hips. They notice your confidence, your smile and whether you listen intently to what they have to say. So wear something that is comfortable yet stylish. Don't go overboard with accessories or fragrance or beauty appointments. Feel comfortable in your own skin and he'll resonate more with you.

From the Male Room

'I don't care what women wear. The only time I care is when they wear something uncomfortable or inappropriate like high heels at a picnic, and then whinge about it.' —**Patrick**

'Having the basic sense to dress appropriately for the occasion is what will mark you as potential girlfriend material. The style, fashion, size, fit and materials are entirely up to you. We don't care. The only other

caveat to this is that if the date involves our boss or
someone else we need to impress professionally, then
we don't want to be embarrassed to be seen with you.
But you really need to try very hard to fail at this. And
we are unlikely to take you somewhere like that in the
early stage of a relationship, anyway.' —**Shaun**

3. Hide your intentions

While you need to listen intently to what men say on
a date, ask follow-up questions and let them do most
of the talking, please know that they not only listen
intently to what *you* have to say, but they watch the
way you act with the eye of a hawk when it comes
to your intentions. Yep, before you even sit down to a
glass of champagne together, he's wondering whether
you're sizing him up as future husband material and if
he even has a slight inkling that you are, he's going to
test you. If you truly are out on the hunt for a husband,
he's going to smell your desperation from a mile away.
He'll pick up on the way you're flirting heavily with
him, or bringing up topics that make you seem like the
perfect wife, or asking questions to suss out his views
on parenting, how many kids he wants or what he
thinks of Hawaii as a honeymoon destination. Do any
of this and don't be surprised if he makes a quick exit
out the back door.

Why are men so afraid of your intentions? A lot
of men innately fear one thing: commitment. They
fear it will ruin their freedom, their sex life and their

manhood as they know it. If you come across even the slightest bit threatening to any of these things on the first date, do not expect a follow-up phone call. Even if he brings up the topic. In fact, *especially* if he brings up the topic. You need to know that it's your job to laugh it off, deflect it and go on to something more interesting. Many men do tests on women to ascertain whether or not she's the type who is looking for a man—any man—to settle with right away. They can smell it. So don't be that girl. (Or at least don't ever let him *think* that you are that girl!)

4. Don't rehearse

There's nothing worse than a woman with a seemingly rehearsed list of questions in her head to ask on a date. Sure, read the newspaper during the day, bring up an interesting film you recently saw or ask him a question about his life aspirations. But don't be rehearsed, rigid or awkward in any way. I know it's easier said than done, but the best way to avoid this is to just be a calmer version of yourself. Talk in a low voice, be demure and classy, don't try too hard and everything will go to plan. If he's not the ideal man for you, don't fret—it was just one date!

5. Be able to hold an intelligent conversation

I'm not telling you that you need to be able to quote the latest stock market options or give your view on the war in Iraq or explain why a stimulus package might be good for the economy. All I'm saying is that when men view you as a woman they could learn something from then their interest—and their nether region—is piqued. Suddenly they not only want to get into your pants, but they'd like to hang out with you, too, because you're interesting. Interesting means that you're well travelled, have passions, goals and dreams (over and above wanting a man) and that your social calendar includes more than man-hunting: the opera, the movies, dance classes, whatever!

If you don't yet have any hobbies or don't do anything other than work and workout, find some. Take on boxing, tennis, learn a language, enrol in a course, make some new friends, go to an art gallery . . . just don't be boring!

From the Male Room

'I can't recall the last time I met a woman who had any interest in cooking—I assume they exist but they must be all taken. In fact, I can't recall any woman that I met in the last few years who had anything that I would call a hobby at all. Does work count? Shopping? Those things don't make a girl interesting at all but that's all women these days seem to want to talk about.'—**Joseph**

6. Listen

Men love to talk. Specifically about themselves. While you might find this boring, imagine what it'd be like for him if he had to listen to you harp on about your period pain or your girlfriend's man problems the entire night! So cut him some slack, listen intently to what he has to say and ask questions pertinent to what he's telling you.

A girlfriend of mine claimed that a guy said she was the best date he had ever had. When I asked her exactly what she did to make a date with her so memorable, she confided to me that she did nothing at all. 'I simply let him speak about himself the *entire time*!'

Enough said.

7. Don't bring up your ex on the date

Every single man I interviewed—yes, 100 per cent of them—have said that when a woman harps on about her ex on the first date, or even mentions him, then she's setting herself up as damaged goods. While it might be an obvious topic of conversation to you, for him it's dead freaking boring. Even if he asks, simply say, 'The past is the past, let's talk about something more interesting.' You may be the first woman ever to have said that to him and he'll be impressed.

8. Don't treat a date as a job interview

While a date might *feel* like a job interview, there's nothing men hate more than when the first question popping out of your mouth is, 'So, what do you do for a living?' Men are extremely sensitive when it comes to what they do for a living, how much money they earn or what their current place in life is. If he is a millionaire then he might feel that you're sizing him up for his cash. If he's poor, he might think you're judging him for not having enough money. You can't win! It's polite to enquire about someone's career, but just be aware of the way you say it and how early on you say it in the conversation.

9. Ditch your mobile

One man once told me that while there's a world of turn-offs out there, your mobile phone is definitely one of the biggest. A woman who spends the entire date checking her text messages or emailing her BFF from her BlackBerry is guaranteed not to get a second date. Put it away for the duration of the date and check your texts once you're done. It's just one hour—you'll survive, I promise!

10. How to end the first date

Saying goodbye is often the trickiest part. But if you keep true to yourself and don't harbour too many expectations, you can do it in style. If you're not interested in a follow-up date, then all you have to do is say, 'It was nice seeing you', kiss him on the cheek or pat him on the back, thank him for dinner and tell him you had a great time. Under no circumstances should you make a promise to see him again. If he asks you when you're free to meet again, say, 'I'm really busy with work in the next few weeks so anything is out of the question till after then.' That should give him the message that you're not keen to repeat the evening.

If you are interested in a follow-up date, don't insist he call you or press the issue. Don't text him straight after the date either. Remember he is the chaser, and that's exactly what he's born to do—chase! And if he liked what he saw, he will.

From the Male Room

'If a woman doesn't come home with me on the first date, I don't feel let down at all. In fact it's quite the opposite! When a woman ends the date first or has somewhere else to go after the date, it makes me more intrigued about her. I definitely will follow up with her because she indicates to me like she's got more going on than just a quest for a boyfriend. Girls who hang around all night are definitely fun, but that's all they are to me—some fun. In the end I don't really take them seriously. It's the ones who are too busy who I want to get to know even more.'—**Richard**

'If the girl ends the date early, it could mean you have not done enough to keep her there or interested; sometimes there can be an empty feeling too and you may not have put enough effort into it. It definitely makes

me want to try harder, not less! In fact I would advise all women that if they want to get a guy interested, or keep him interested, they should always end the date first and not hang around all night.'—**Wayne**

'I like communication. I think women should take the initiative at least 20 per cent of the time. But that's about all. Women can easily go overboard and get into lengthy text or email conversations. As men we don't really get off on that. In fact it makes us really bored with you really quickly.'—**Trent**

11. Always offer to pay!

A whopping 70 per cent of men (from my Great Man Survey of two thousand men) say they want to pay for the first date but would prefer the woman to offer. So doing the cursory wallet-grab isn't such a bad idea. Just make sure you actually have some cash in there in case he accepts!

12. A word about sex on the first date

Despite the amount of data on the subject, a question I so often get asked is whether a woman should sleep with a guy on the first date.

'But what if I want it just as much as he does?' many women ask me. 'Some men say it doesn't make a difference!' they insist.

But here's the catch: of course men are going to tell you that it doesn't make a difference. Of course they are going to do/say/buy anything to get you into the sack as soon as possible. But if you're serious about your date, or your future with this guy (and even if you're not), it's always a better idea to avoid the repercussions that come with sleeping with a guy too soon.

Be aware that 67.1 per cent of men from my Great Man Survey say if they sleep with you on the first date and say they really like you but don't call, they weren't that into you in the first place and were only after one thing. So don't be fooled! You don't need to give him a line like, 'I don't normally do this, but you're different,' because he's heard it before. In fact, many men I've polled simply laugh to themselves at this line and applaud their efforts for being able to get laid so soon!

A better tactic is to put a big cheeky smile on your face and tell him this: 'I like to take things slow.' That way he knows that he needs to work doubly hard for your affections; not because you're a prude or you're scared of sex or you're not a modern woman, but because you're a modern woman who's learned from her past and is in complete control of her destiny. Now what man wouldn't want a woman like that?

13. Chill the fuck out after the first date

Urgh, the day after the first date. You felt the butterflies, you saw the sparkle in his eyes, he told you about his mum and now you're totally into him and think he could be 'the one'. Visions of marriage and babies start floating through your mind and, before you know it, you've mentally moved your wardrobe into his abode, met his parents and impressed his friends. Well, back off, Cleopatra. It was just one date.

This is fantasy jumping. Even if he was the most charming, charismatic bloke you've ever met who promised you a trip to the Caribbean and commitment for life, know that actions speak louder than words. At least wait for the follow-up phone call before you start picking out baby names, because there's no point in obsessing over a man who isn't into you. No. Freaking. Point.

Oh, and about waiting for that elusive follow-up phone call? A word of advice: men don't see things—particularly time—the same way women do. So what happens is that after the first date, he doesn't even think about you. He plays sport, goes to work, sees his mates, and then come day three, four or five, or even a few weeks, and he might suddenly think, 'Oh wow! I haven't heard from Sam—I wonder what she's up to!' And then *wham*—his chase instinct kicks in. He calls. Or texts. You play it aloof, cool, flirty, fun and are happy to hear from him. You are chilled. You have been busy. But you accept a second date at a time *that suits you*. He thinks you're the most chilled-out, relaxed girl he's ever met and he can't believe his luck that he's finally found a woman who isn't so clingy after just one freaking date!

There is no need to punish men who don't call. There is also no need to text or call them before they call you. In fact, it's date suicide. Because suddenly they're thinking, 'Gee, this woman is rather desperate—I'm not that interested!'

Instead, give him a chance to miss you. Or at least remember you exist. Trust the process. It works every time.

14. The call diary

So, you refused to listen to my sound advice about not calling him and found your hand reaching towards your mobile without your brain being able to stop it? And now you feel like a fool because he hasn't called, texted or emailed you back. It's been three whole hours and you can't stop yourself staring at your mobile or checking that it still works. It does work. So breathe, put it away in a drawer and go for a run or do some laundry. If you want to prevent this situation from happening again, then you need to keep a call diary. Here's what I want you to do right now, this minute. Grab a piece of paper and write down these words:

> I have just texted/called/emailed [insert date's name here] and I feel like an idiot/a moron/hopeless/rejected. I definitely should not have done it. Therefore, next time I am in this predicament I will *not* do any of the above. I will remember how I'm feeling right at this moment and know that I don't want to experience it ever again. I am worth more than this. I will not chase men.

Stick it up on your wall or on your mirror and stare at it until it sinks in. Most importantly, *stop* making stupid excuses for him. If a man likes you, he'll call you. End of story.

When he *does* text/call/email you, repeat the exercise before you even think about responding. How do you feel now? I bet you feel in control, on top of the world, like you hold all the power—which you do, since you're no longer the one doing the chasing. Which is exactly how I want you to feel *all the time*.

From the Male Room

'*If a girl doesn't text me back straightaway, I assume she's busy at work. I'm not concerned. Texting is not an instantaneous medium. I knew a woman who had free text and would try to conduct long conversations by text. It's annoying when you are working and paying 27 cents per text. If you need to actually discuss something, use the phone! But if women don't reply to a text according to some kind of "rules", I tend to get annoyed. If I text you at noon asking you out for a drink after work, then I understand you may be in a meeting and may not respond for several hours. But don't blame me if it is now 7:30 pm and I have gone home and you reply saying yes. Your "meeting" didn't last that long. I don't mind that you didn't reply, but don't try to turn it into being my fault.*'—**Ben**

15. The myth of the third-date rule

The unspoken truth of first dates is that the man pays, the woman is paid for and all is right and balanced in the world. The male attempts to court the female, willingly proffering up his hard-earned dollars in a bid to impress her. More recently, however, with the proliferation of the third-date rule—which stipulates that the two of you are supposed to sleep together on the third date—he knows that he won't be putting down the dough for too long before he gets the opportunity to jump into your pants. He simply pays for three dates and you sleep with him on the third, or it's over.

If you don't like the sound of this, perhaps you should adhere to the rule I give all women wanting a free dinner: *If you don't intend to sleep with the bloke, always pay your share.* I'm serious. The third-date rule is rampant so if you're not ready for sex, don't get caught in the trap.

The way to avoid the third-date pitfall is to do the following from dates one through to three:

- Don't put yourself in situations where you find yourself alone, back at his house.
- Don't agree to watch a DVD at your place or his.
- Don't accept to see him after 10 pm.
- Keep the dates to a maximum of three hours.

Take the sad tale of Janelle, who ignored my sage advice and allowed the guy to pay on the third date anyway, despite having no intention of getting into bed with him. When it came time to drop her home, he casually mentioned that they'd both be heading back to his place. When she refused, he simply opened the car door, kicked her out and drove off. Just like that. Left her on the street to find her own way home. While most men wouldn't dream of being so callous, there's a lesson to be learned when it comes to giving people false expectations.

If you are ready to do the horizontal hanky-panky on the third date, then by all means go ahead. Just know that this doesn't necessarily mean it's going to go anywhere serious yet. Chances are he's just waiting around to get you into the sack. You know the signs by now. And you also know that you don't have to be pressured into anything you don't want to do. Or anything that you think will jeopardise your power. Which means that if you fall in love with him after sleeping with him too soon, but he hasn't yet fallen in love with you, you're going to be heartbroken. So don't do it! Wait until you are ready, take as much time as you need and remember, it takes a minimum of three months to really get to know someone, not three dates!

16. Acting slightly innocent

While The Catch is definitely not a virgin, she makes the utmost effort to come across as extremely classy and hard to get into the sack. She makes herself sound elusive, unavailable and someone men have to fight for in order to get her to let her guard down and get naked with them. She might be having sex with her booty buddy later that night, but as far as her date is concerned, she doesn't talk crudely about sex, she isn't 'up for it' before the time is right and she doesn't often have men stay over at her house. She has had only a few sexual partners and never has one-night stands. And she hasn't tried every single sexual position in the Kama Sutra either.

Remember, it doesn't really matter if The Catch has or hasn't done any of these things, but the key is that she doesn't let the man she's seeing in on her secret . . . ever. She encourages him to feel he is special for being allowed to see her naked; not that he is just another notch on her belt or that she lets every man she meets get their rocks off with her. The Catch doesn't see this as playing games or manipulating men either— she sees it as an investment in her future. A man always treats a woman with more respect and wants to woo her if he feels that he's getting special privileges by playing his cards right. He will feel as though she is the ultimate prize—The Catch—and he will work harder to get her and appreciate her more once he has her.

Remember:
Men are visual creatures
Men are definitely visual creatures, so pull out all the stops on a date. By that, I don't mean showing off your cleavage, your legs and every inch of your body. Oh no.

You're not handing yourself to him on a platter. You're simply looking elegant and sexy at the same time.

Order a beer

Men are giving you a test on the date, so why not pass it right away? The men I date usually sit down and order a beer. Sometimes, if I'm really trying to pass his tests, I'll simply say, 'I'll have one, too.' You should see the shock flash across his face!

Eat a burger

Men will look very carefully at what you eat on the date, so it's not a bad idea to just order something that you might not usually eat on a daily basis. Why not have some fun with it? Theresa does this flawlessly. Every time she goes on a date with a man she really likes, she always orders the burger. She doesn't eat all of it, but she picks a bit at the meat and the salad. He doesn't notice exactly what she eats because he's still so impressed that she actually ordered the burger that he's staring mindlessly into her eyes! And she always gets asked out on a second date.

Knowing about the news

Men often tell me that it's so hard to find a woman these days who is both smart and pretty. There are women who are so busy they don't bother with things like world affairs, local news, business, the economy or anything other than their job, girlfriends, dating life and interests like beauty, fashion, reality TV, whatever. But if you really want to get a second look-in from a guy you're keen on, hop online and read the news. It only takes a few minutes. I like to read the *New York Times* online and make sure that I'm abreast with what's going on with politics, world affairs and definitely in business news. It might sound boring, but it's actually rather fascinating learning what companies are doing, who they're buying, what stocks are doing well and who's just been arrested for insider trading. Plus, the men I meet are completely on top of it all, which means that I always have something to talk to them about when we go on a date. And men love nothing more than to be asked for help, so I always am able to ask them to explain something in detail to me and they happily oblige! I'm not sure what it is about a woman being able to speak about news, politics and business to a man, but if you want a second date, the secret is to remember three news stories that caught your interest and to have an interesting point of view about each one, but also have some questions in mind that you are able to ask your date.

Knowing about sport
I know, I know . . . there are many of you out there who like nothing less than to talk about sport. I'm not saying that you need to actually watch every single game on television, but by having a broad knowledge of what games are on, what teams are playing and when

the next big worldwide sporting event is going to take place, it makes you a more interesting date. In fact, bringing up sport with a man by asking him about his favourite team, if he watched the game or what he thinks of a certain player switching teams, suddenly makes him pay attention.

From the Male Room

> *'Whenever I hear a woman talk about sports or that she watched "the game" or that she knows the names of one of the players, my ears suddenly perk up. She's definitely suddenly girlfriend material in my mind! I don't need her to sit and watch the game with me every Friday night. I understand that is a guy thing. But it would be nice once in a while for her to acknowledge just how important sport is for us men.'*—**Dean**

> *'Exercise like anyone else and enjoy a bloody chocolate ice-cream instead of a stupid herbal tea and some celery sticks. Then we'll take you out again.'*—**Lyle**

Don't reveal too much about yourself
Keep an air of mystery about yourself. You don't want to tell him everything just yet. After all, you're not even sure you like him! Save a few personal things about yourself for when you're actually in a relationship.

Don't have any expectations at the end

At the end of the date, politely thank him for the date and don't ask if he's going to call you or whether or not he likes you. Take the time to watch his actions following the date. Ask yourself if you like *him*! Ask yourself what you think about him and whether or not he is the type of guy you want to get to know a little better.

More first-date tips:

- Thank him, but don't dote on him for paying. Getting to spend time with you is reward enough.
- Never answer your phone on a date (unless you need an 'out').
- Don't tell him if you have another date planned later that night, that week, that month—whatever. At least make him feel special for just that one night.

12
Playing by the rules

The Catch strategy

I always thought that my friend Cathy was a natural with men; she's a total Catch. I would watch in awe as the men would all clamour for her attention, every single time we headed out. And even when we weren't out together, men would call me up and ask me if she was available. The men she actually dates are usually of some sort of celebrity status, always super hot and are always fighting for her attentions. They never get bored; she does. So what's her secret? She sticks to some rules.

She's busy

'Even if I desperately want to see a guy, I tell them that I have plans just occasionally and that they'll have to schedule in another time to see me.' The Catch always makes sure that she has tonnes of things going on and tonnes of interesting people to do things with. She is never bored or lonely and definitely not always available for a guy.

From the Male Room

'I would usually leave it for about a week but no longer than two weeks with either a text message or an email. Some girls will try and contact me the next day or a few days later asking where I've been. I've been at work!'—**Ken**

'I don't mind if a woman texts me after a date but it can be a bit too much sometimes. I usually just tell her that I had a great night and we will talk soon. I'll admit I have had my fair share of women who have just been unbearable and sent a few too many text messages and I admit I have done that myself with women I liked and stuffed things up too.'— **Eugene**

She makes him work for it

The Catch has a few hoops that she likes men to jump through before she'll give them any rewards. (And by rewards, I'm talking about things like texts, calls, saying 'yes' to dates—not sexual favours!) One interesting story Cathy told me about happened when she started dating her current boyfriend, a super celebrity. She told him she was heading out to the country to meet with some friends. Oddly enough, he said he was going that way too and asked if she'd like meet up there. The place they were both visiting was over an hour away. She said sure and told him to call her on his way.

Cathy drove to the country, met up with her friends, did some shopping, ate lunch and still hadn't heard from the celebrity. But instead of sending him a text, calling him, emailing him, Facebooking him or tweeting him, she made a conscious decision to do nothing, except drive back home to the city.

Just as she got home, he called.

'Hey, I'm here,' he said.

'Oh, too bad,' she replied. 'I'm already home.'

She never complained that he didn't call or text her to let her know he was on his way. She simply said 'Too bad' and then left it alone.

'Well, am I going to have to start chasing you all around the city now?' he asked.

'You might have to!' she said brightly.

When Cathy told me the story, I was quite taken aback. Here is a super celebrity who can have any girl in the entire country he wants. He must have women throwing themselves at him from every single angle and most likely never, ever has to work at getting a woman's affections. It must just all come so easy to him! And yet here he was, driving around for hours, chasing my friend all over various parts of the city, just so he could spend some time with her! Yes, this is the power of The Catch.

The takeaway from this is that Catches always have their own lives that are exciting, fulfilling, busy, awesome, enjoyable and fun. They are never the ones chasing after men; the men are the ones after them. He wants to be a part of her awesome world, and he needs to prove to her that he's worthy of it.

She doesn't take his shit . . . but ignores it rather than nagging about it

All men give women little tests to see how they'll react. They attempt bad behaviour, which involves not communicating when they said they would, not paying for a date, forgetting an important date or cancelling plans at the last minute. The Catch doesn't accept this bad behaviour. But she doesn't berate a man over it either. If a man tosses one of these tests her way, she completely ignores him. Silence is golden. She doesn't say 'It's OK', or that she's disappointed as she was hoping to hear from him. Nor does she ask him where he's been or what (or who) he's been doing or why he cancelled/didn't do what he promised he'd do. She just simply reads his cancellation text or listens to his excuses on voicemail, and then she makes other plans, plants a smile on her face and walks out the door. She doesn't give it another thought, nor does she dwell on it. When he tries to contact her later that night or the next day, she's still busy. And so he begins to wonder if perhaps he did the wrong thing; if perhaps she's slipping out of his grasp; if he has to work harder to gain her attentions—if he has to spring back into chase mode. And he does because she shows men—in only her actions and without any words—that what they've done is wrong and that she won't actually accept this sort of behaviour. They never do it again. And if they do, The Catch ceases contact with them for good.

She doesn't give to her date . . . at least not until she feels he deserves it

Too many women feel that the way to a man's heart is to give to him. I'm talking about presents, text messages, lifts, paying for things he needs because he 'can't afford it'—you name it, these girls like to give it. But what ends up happening is that he stops seeing her as someone he has to chase, and he starts seeing her as someone he can use to get his needs fulfilled. No-one in a 'dating' situation wants to end up like that. It ruins any chance at chemistry. Women often complain to me that they spent all this money and time getting a man the perfect gift for his birthday or their anniversary, or whatever it is, but when they give it to him, he hardly glances at it, doesn't say thank you and barely acknowledges all the effort they put into giving it to him. You see, while women like men the more they give, the opposite is the case for men. The more a woman gives to him, the more he believes that he's done enough to have 'earned' her gifts, and the less he feels he has to do.

Seriously, women have to do absolutely nothing to get a man's attention during the courtship and dating stage. If you want to be seen as a Catch, *do nothing*. Don't buy him things, nor make a humongous effort to plan the perfect date; don't try too hard to impress him. Let him do all the work. You'd be surprised at how hard he'll try as soon as you sit back and let him woo you. Biologically, men are hardwired to do this . . . so why ruin all their fun?

She is always prepared to walk away

When things aren't going The Catch's way with a new man and he isn't calling or texting her as much as she'd like, instead of waiting around like a lovesick puppy or beating herself up over it before questioning why he's MIA, she simply gets ready to walk away. If a man isn't showing that he is truly into her, she ends it. She has no time or patience to chase after a man who is not 100 per cent into her. What for, when there are, like, five other guys waiting in the wings?

The funny thing about The Catch's actions in this scenario is that when she's not getting what she wants out of a man, she either simply stops contacting them or replying to their attempts to contact her, or she tells them that she's no longer interested. 'Let's just be friends,' she tells them. And it works every time: the guy comes grovelling back, and never makes the same faux pas again. The lesson here is that you want to project the attitude that you don't *need* a man. You were fine before he came along, and you'll be fine when he leaves. Your life hasn't dramatically changed since he entered it. In fact, it was pretty darn good before. It's just that now he's the icing on the cake—someone you can have fun with a couple of times a week. He is not the answer. He is not the solution to any of your problems. He solves nothing. And he should know that he is lucky to be a part of your life, but that you could do without him!

It's never her fault

The Catch knows that she never has to blame herself or let her self-esteem go down the gurgler when a man disappoints her or doesn't live up to his promises or her expectations. Because she knows that relationships and commitment are reliant on myriad factors, and that these are mostly contingent on things that are out of her control. These include life stage, timing, the status of his last relationship, his career, his work, his family . . . She knows she's a Catch and she never lets the behaviour of a man determine whether or not she fully believes this.

How men react to The Catch strategy

Like it or not, the male reaction to The Catch strategy is biological. Certain receptors in his brain fire off when you follow it to the letter and if a man is going to back off because you're not texting, calling him all the time or sleeping with him right away, then good riddance. You are weeding out the ones that aren't worthy of you anyway! The problem is that when you do meet a good one, if you go off script you risk scaring him off or pushing him away prematurely. The Catch understands the way men react and the way they see themselves, and therefore does not risk desperate Toss girl behaviour!

Men biologically need to 'defend their turf'

Another way men work biologically is that part of their brain that controls their instinctive need to defend their turf. This area—the dorsal pre-mammillary nucleus—is, according to brain expert Louann Brizendine, larger in the male brain and contains special circuits to detect territorial challenges by other males.[8] In other words, the more suitors who are chasing after The Catch, the more he senses that she is indeed a Catch, and the more he wants to chase her. The Catch knows that it's important to have many men chasing her at once so that she doesn't have time to put all her focus on one man, or to worry about when (or if) he's going to call so that she comes across as too needy. She isn't—she's too busy fending off (or giving a chance to) the others, to notice.

> **#40. ALWAYS DATE A FEW MEN UNTIL ONE STEPS IT UP ENOUGH TO DESERVE YOUR COMMITMENT**
>
> Men sense when you have other men around you and they'll do anything to compete to get your attention. Make sure you are dating a few men to encourage the healthy competition men crave.

Men always look at the beginning of the relationship as just fun

Remember this important point: while you're sizing up a new date as potential husband material, he's thinking how great that exact moment being with you is. He's not thinking about the future, how many kids you'll have or what kind of house the two of you will live in. Women who see themselves as The Catch do exactly the same thing. They give men the chance to enjoy their company without projecting their entire future lives onto him.

From the Male Room

*'I never tell a girl that we are in a relationship. Instead,
I make a girl feel exclusive when I begin to take more*

interest in her, like buying her gifts, and planning stuff
that would surprise her. Hopefully she will pick up
on it without us having to have a conversation about
it.'—**Wayne**

♥ #41. HAVE FUN WITH THE DATING
PROCESS

You don't need to be too serious at the
beginning of the relationship. This is your
time to get to know him and to judge whether
or not you want to get to know him even
better.

His job comes first—before cuddles, sex and you

Steve Harvey, author of *Act Like a Lady, Think Like a
Man*, helped me understand the connection between
a man and his job.[9] In the very first few pages of his
book, he explains that, until a man has a title, job and
income he's proud of, he'll never be the man you want
him to be.

He says that if men aren't pursuing their dreams
or don't have their ducks in a row, they feel 'doomed'.
And until they find that, you are never going to be top
priority. So don't even try.

> ### ♥ #42. DON'T DATE AN UNSTABLE MAN
>
> When a man doesn't have a stable job or feels he isn't earning enough income to support you, he will pull away. You will be left feeling lonely and unloved. Don't do it to yourself. He is not the man for you.

They know when you're desperate . . . for their hand in marriage

Men can't ask for directions or pick up their underwear, but there's one thing they're more intuitive about than anything else: a woman who is desperate. If husband hunting is a sport more appealing to you than AFL or bargain shopping, then you'd better find a way to see relationships as men do: as accessories and vacations, not entire careers.

From the Male Room

'The best thing for a woman to say about her relationship status is that she is open to discussion. She should not talk too much about the romps she has had. I guess she could talk about dating disasters or something that is funny. But definitely no talk about her ex—that is a deal breaker!'—**Ted**

'If a woman says she is looking for a boyfriend, it may depend on how she says it. She could be saying that

she would like a boyfriend who will treat her well and be there for her. Maybe she has had some disasters and she is not just looking for sex! Some women could say it out of desperation or maybe she is looking for a rebound relationship. I think it's best not to say anything and if a guy asks what you are looking for, say something like you haven't really thought about it. This will make him want to try harder and not think you are just desperate for any man to fill the role of a boyfriend.'—**Jonathan**

'As men we don't like to be thought of as someone who can just slot into a woman's five-year plan. We want them to actually like us for us. And we know when we're just being used as part of their mission to get married. My ex-girlfriend was like that. She would always tell me her wedding plans, and when I told her I wasn't ready, she didn't care and went ahead with things anyway. It was weird, but looking back on it I can see very clearly that she didn't really care whether or not it was me or another guy—she just wanted her dream wedding and that was it.'—**Adrian**

 #43. NEVER HAVE MARRIAGE ON YOUR MIND WITH A NEW MAN

He will sense it from a mile away and he'll take full advantage of you then toss you aside before dessert.

You don't need new red lacy underwear for the first night

Here's a newsflash: men don't know the difference between whether you've just dropped a small fortune on La Perla or you've bought your goods from Target. Better yet, as 100 per cent of the men I polled responded: 'No underwear would make life a whole lot easier.'

Never believe what a man says when sex is on the cards

OK ladies, I have no doubt you're sick to death of hearing that it's imperative to make a man wait to have sex with you. Author Steve Harvey reckons the time to make him wait is three months, and to not let him have it any sooner. Some men say it's after three dates. And most dudes will tell you it doesn't matter when you do it with them, as long as it's done as early on as possible. But *of course* they're going to tell *you* that; after all, men just want to get laid! And there's nothing wrong with that either. In fact I'd be rather worried if you were seeing a man who really didn't want to have sex with you any time soon. He's a man; he wants to have sex as quickly and as cheaply as possible. His testosterone tells him to go out and get it.

But guess what? His testosterone has nothing to do with him wanting to treat you well, committing to you or seeing you as a long-term prospect. Nothing.

So if you satiate the desires of his testosterone, all that will happen is his ability to see you as The Catch will evaporate. It will *no longer exist*. He'll be thinking solely with his dick. End of story. So, what's The Catch to do? It's not simple, but it's effective, so listen up.

It's likely that at some point the thought of having sex with you will cross his mind. He's not thinking of marrying you or whether you'd make a good girl-friend or a great spag bol. He may wonder when he's going to get laid. If you put this off, you start to enable him to see you for more than just a vagina. He starts to look at the other aspects of you. He starts to be able to *fall in love with you*.

Generally, a man takes around three to four months to fall in love with a woman. And falling in love for a man isn't through sex. For women, yes. When you sleep with a man—no matter how long you've known him—you will instantly develop more feelings for him than you had before you slept with him. You will start to see him as more of a long-term prospect. That is how our brains work. Him—the opposite. He doesn't want to think of his future wife or the mother of his kids as a woman who jumps into bed with every man she meets. He just doesn't. But that doesn't mean he won't try. So, what's a girl to do?

From the Male Room

'Seriously girls need to slow down! It takes me about six months after knowing the person well enough to

fall in love, and also your heart has to be in it. Too many girls are too quick to want to say "I love you". It's weird, creepy and makes me want to dump her immediately.'—**Joseph**

Here are some rules:

- If he pressures you into sex early on, unless that's all you want (and be honest with yourself!), then walk away. It's not worth it. Just because he tells you that by sleeping with him your relationship will improve and go to the next level, doesn't mean it's true. Men will do and say anything to get you into bed. Especially lie.

- If you find yourself in a compromising situation where you are back at his house or he is back at your house, it's perfectly OK for you to tell him that you want to wait. If he is the right guy for you, he will respect that. You can say the following:

    ★ 'I think you're awesome, and I don't see the point in rushing things just yet.'

    ★ 'Wow, it's getting hot in here. Let's stop and take a walk, don't you think?'

    ★ 'I really want to have sex with you. But not tonight. What do you think about waiting a few weeks?'

    ★ 'I'd love to have sex with you right now, but

in the past it hasn't ended very well when I've rushed things. I'd like to wait a little while first. Is that OK with you?' Of course if he says it's not OK with him, then you are within your rights to exit the situation straightaway. And you should.

- If you think that he's only in it for one thing, you can casually ask him if he's ever had a one-night stand, and how he felt about it. Usually men who are emotionally in tune with you will tell you that it wasn't that fun and that he prefers to have sex with someone he actually cares about. Then you can say 'Me too', and once that conversation has been had in an environment in which you are both fully clothed, it will make it easier when the time comes close to remember what he said about the other woman he had a one-night stand with, and to make sure that you don't let yourself fall into that category.

- It's important to have some sort of a conversation about when he was last tested and what kind of protection he likes to use before you sleep with him. There is nothing worse than being in the moment and then having the guy refuse to use a condom, then making you feel guilty about wanting to, then going ahead anyway and fearing afterwards that you are pregnant or have an STD or both.

From the Male Room

'Sleeping with a girl could depend on the mood and if there is sexual chemistry there. I usually give it one to three months and if nothing happens then it's best to reconsider your options—we all have sexual needs too! That being said, I have waited for sex with other women I have been friends with and to be honest it was worth the wait.'—**Michael**

'Ninety-nine per cent of men definitely lie, cheat or steal or would throw their mothers in front of a bus to get laid.'—**Jake**

'Men will sell their souls to the devil to get it!'
—**Robert**

After you have sex with him

In the time of the booty call buddy and the casual sex generation, women are still getting confused by how men can have sex without emotional consequences while you may not. Don't let your boundaries fly out the window. Even Lady Gaga has renounced sex, saying it's unnecessary until the right person comes along. At least that's a start.

The thing most men complain to me about is the fact that women change after sex. They say most women become needy and start expecting more from a man once she gives it up. She expects phone calls and text messages and for him to see her all the time.

The man, on the other hand, does the opposite. He pulls back. He's got what he wanted, now he wants to know the answer to the ultimate question: 'What else you got?' Sure, you can give a good blow job. But then again, so can every other girl who is after him. He wants to ascertain what else you can do. Can you cook? Do you know anything about guy hobbies? Are you fun? Do you like doing interesting things? Do you appreciate him? All these things are what he will now be looking closely at. The other thing he'll be watching for extremely closely is how much you change. So, you need to be counter-intuitive after sex. And you need to actually *pull back* rather than push forward. Just because you had sex it does *not* mean you are suddenly in a relationship. You are not. And until you have that conversation, neither of you are obliged not to see other people.

Annabelle was extremely smart about this. After she had sex with Mark for the first time—she waited a month before they did it—she decided that she was not only *not* going to change, but she was going to make sure that he didn't think she was going to suddenly become clingy. And so she specifically told him that just because they'd had sex, it did not mean anything until they had the conversation. She phrased it like this: 'Do you think once people have sex they should stop seeing other people?' She didn't tell him what to do nor make any demands. She maintained her Catch persona and remained cool and not needy. And Mark immediately jumped in: 'Well, I don't want you having sex with anyone else now.' He didn't even ask her if it was OK with her, he just said it. And she was happy, because hopefully that meant that he would not be having sex with other people.

She could have jumped in and told him that she expected the same of him, but the truth was they had only been dating for one month. And she rationalised that if he liked her enough, and didn't want to hurt her, then he wouldn't be sleeping with other people. So instead of telling him not to sleep with other people, she said: 'OK, well I don't expect anything from you at this point. But I do not want to get hurt. So if you do decide to sleep with someone else, I need you to tell me so that I can move on.' He didn't sleep with anyone else, and they are now—six months on—happily engaged.

What Annabelle did well was that she didn't equate sleeping with him as being in love with him. Not for one second. Instead, she told herself to separate the act from the forward-motion of the relationship. But she did—in different words—tell Mark that if he wanted to fuck around, then he was kaput. Since she views herself as a Catch, she doesn't want to be with a man who a) isn't honest, and b) is sleeping with other women while sleeping with her. She used language and phrasing which made it clear to, but was not directed at, Mark. And it worked like a charm.

#44. SEX DOES NOT EQUAL LOVE

Even if you're the most sexually liberated woman ever, having sex with a man who isn't yet committed to you will still make you weaker. The Catch only does things to make herself stronger, and if that means eradicating casual sex from her diet, then so be it.

Part 4

The First
Three Months

A Cautionary Tale: Camilla

'Will you come and meet my new flatmates?' Camilla begged Kate as she swung her Chanel handbag over her shoulder. She'd been staying in that dingy apartment for long enough and would often sleep on Kate's couch to avoid having to go there at all. But while she knew her friend adored having the company, she also knew she was wearing out her welcome—fast. So naturally Kate was delighted that Camilla was finally getting a proper place she could permanently call home.

'Er, do you think I'd let you bunker up with strangers without me getting to meet them first? Seriously, you met them online. They could be serial killers!'

Camilla giggled. 'Nah, I've met Tracey already. She's awesome!'

Tracey, the girl who had put out the ad looking for flatmates, had organised Friday night drinks for all three tenants to meet one another before they moved in the following week.

'She told me she's got a boyfriend and she says she's always travelling for work, so she'll hardly ever be there! And there's a guy, too, who I haven't met yet, but Tracey says he's gay, so there's nothing to worry about. I can't imagine having to live with a straight guy any time soon.' Camilla shuddered. The last thing she wanted right now was to live with another man. She hadn't lived with one since she moved out of Mr Ex's place, and she wasn't about to jump headfirst *another domestic living arrangement. The fact her new flatmate was gay helped, sort of.*

As the two girls headed to the bar, Camilla stopped on the sidewalk, watching a tall, handsome guy walking in.

'Cute!' she hissed, noticing he looked just like Ashton Kutcher.

'No boy talk!' Kate shot back. 'You promised!'

'I can look, can't I? I'm not touching!' Camilla hit Kate playfully on the arm.

As they walked into the bar, Camilla noticed Tracey sitting on a stool at the back. And then she saw the Mr Kutcher lookalike she'd noticed before walking right up to Tracey! And passing her a drink! God, how dumb am I? *Camilla thought.* That's Tracey's boyfriend! I can't be lusting after my new flatmate's boyfriend! What a terrible start.

As Camilla and Kate made their way towards Tracey and 'Mr Kutcher', Camilla felt herself blushing. He was just so bloody cute. Argh. Why couldn't she find herself a man like that? Seriously? Sure, Tracey was pretty and all, and super sweet, so she probably deserved him. But what about me? *Camilla thought.* When is this crazy douchebag spell going to end?

Just as they were approaching, Tracey noticed them and her smile broadened.

'Hey, roomy!' she yelled out to Camilla, waving her hand in the air. 'And you must be Kate?' She got up to give Kate a big bear hug. 'Cam has told me so much about you! And this,' she said, turning to point at Mr Kutcher, 'is

our other new flatmate—Kade! Kade meet Camilla, Camilla meet Kade.'

OK, now he is sooo not gay, *Camilla thought. So not gay!* Fuck, fuck, fuck. This is not good. *She couldn't stop thinking how dangerous it would be to have a crush on your flatmate! In fact, one minute into their conversation, Cam knew that Kade was definitely, definitely* not gay. *And worse, he was just her type: he had an intelligent, interesting face, and looked kind of shy too, in an endearing sort of non-arrogant way.*

Damn. What the hell had she gotten herself into?

When Kade eventually got up to go to the bathroom, Camilla confronted her new flatmate, 'What the hell? You said he was gay!'

'I know, babe,' *said Tracey, shrugging her shoulders.* 'Knew you would never accept it if he was straight. And I really wanted you to move in. Had to lie. Soz, babe!'

And with that Kade was back. And Camilla was once again staring into his deliciously velvet brown eyes.

13

Guy Time: The first three to four months

I often get asked by women, 'I want him to tell me where this is going—I want him to tell me what he thinks of me—if he likes me—if he sees me in his future . . . how should I say it?' Well, back up for just a minute, sister. You want him to make all those decisions right now? After only two weeks/one month/two months? Oh no.

What about *your* decisions? Here's how you look at it from now on. *You* are sizing him up. He has to prove his worth to you. You want a boyfriend, but you're also picky and have standards and codes of ethics and behaviour. If he doesn't come up to these, then *you don't want him in your future*. What for, when there is another man around the corner who will have the qualities you are really after? Why stand for crap when gold is just around the bend? Why waste your, energy and precious time when you could be exercising, working, seeing your friends, building an empire—working on yourself?

If you are struggling to get him to commit, back off. It's not the right time for you. Something in your powerful woman scenario is not adding up. The other fact is that men need at least three to four months of processing information in their heads in order to even *start* to realise they want to see a woman as part of their future. Too many women jump the gun during this phase, which relationship and dating expert John Gray calls the 'uncertainty' phase.[10] But he stipulates that while a man might pull back and perhaps even stop calling or texting you during this phase, he is only doing this because he is uncertain and he needs some Guy Time.

Guy Time . . . which doesn't include you

If you learn anything from this book, know this: guy time is the time a guy takes out away from you with no contact whatsoever. This doesn't mean that he doesn't like you—it means that he is processing things in his head. If you interrupt guy time by contacting him or asking him why he has gone cold, it will make him think that you are no longer The Catch. He will suddenly view you as needy, desperate and not the woman for him.

Some men need a few days of guy time here and there, others can take months. It's highly frustr for all of us to have to sit through guy time and wait, and wait, and wait some more for him to come around. But as John Gray says, men are like rubber bands. When they pull away, they will always come springing back, unless you do something to cut their rubber band. Things you can do to instantly cut their rubber band so that they are gone for good include the following:

- Asking him, 'Where have you gone? Why are you ignoring me?'
- Asking him if something is wrong.
- Asking him if he is seeing other people.
- Questioning his affections for you.
- Telling him that you expect more from the relationship and that if he is not going to give it to you, then 'see you later'.
- Poking him on Facebook.
- Stalking him on Facebook and then berating him for talking to other women.
- Stalking him when he is out with his friends.
- Asking him to spend more time with you.
- Calling or texting him 'just to say hi'.

While women communicate with each other on a regular basis for no particular reason whatsoever, men aren't built like us. They don't value this sort of communication and think that if you attempt this with him, then you are not a Catch, but instead are high maintenance and too much work. They want things as seamless and easy as possible. If you make things difficult, he will not be impressed.

Subsequently, when he finally emerges from guy time and wants to see you or contacts you, you are allowed to be busy on the exact time or day he wants to see you, because you are not sitting around waiting for him. But at the same time, you are still happy to hear from him and you show him that you are such a confident, together, non-desperate, non-needy woman that you're OK with him retreating into his guy time whenever he needs to do so.

Of course this happens less and less after the four-month mark when he finally decides to make a commitment to you. But you don't allow him to think it was his decision because you always make out like you're the one sizing him up until you are both ready to take things to the next level. Also, never think that by offering sex, he is going to come out of guy time. He is—but only for a nanosecond. If you let him think of you as someone who satiates his sexual urges without him making a proper effort or giving to you, he is going to cease seeing you as The Catch.

How to go from casual dating to commitment

The biggest question I get asked by women is how to get a man to commit. Firstly, let's define exactly what commitment looks like:

- He is dating you—exclusively.
- He calls you his girlfriend in public.
- He introduces you to his friends and family.
- He starts discussing the future with you.

But way before you decide that this is the man who you actually *want* to commit to you, you need to test him just a little. The Catch does this flawlessly by asking the men she's interested in a few questions (but not on the first date!).

From the Male Room

'I will commit to a girl for the long haul when she can demonstrate to me that she has the capacity not to be a drama queen, that she doesn't withhold sex as a bargaining chip and that she understands the difference between income and expenditure. I don't mind if you don't want to work, but don't expect to live like a double-income couple if that is your choice. And one other tip. It is always unwise to provoke an argument with a man with a full bladder. Wait until he visits the bathroom first.'—**Jake**

Questions to ask a man to gauge whether he's the commitment type

- Ask why his last relationship broke off and how long it lasted.
- Ask him to define commitment.
- Ask him how long it usually takes him to commit to a woman.

From the Male Room

'It takes a year for me to want to commit. After about six to eight months I start to feel guilty that I've spent so much time with this girl and therefore I start to talk to her about the future. And I just hope to god she doesn't bring it up before I do.'—**Harry**

Girlfriend material versus one night (or months) of fun . . .

For months, I found myself in so-called relationships with men who were only up for one thing: 'fun'. Whenever I'd question their level of commitment, they'd often laugh and then tell me that I was acting too serious. 'What do you mean? We're just having fun.'

Argh . . . that word again. For a while I wondered what was wrong with me. Was I the girl who men only wanted to have fun with and never took seriously? What kind of message was I putting across to them that signalled that I was the 'just for fun' girl? The Friday-night-sex girl? I thought I was doing everything right! I didn't sleep with them too soon, didn't act needy or desperate (or so I thought) and didn't pressure them into a relationship. So why weren't they clamouring to make me their girlfriend? Why did they never bring up commitment?

And then I realised the problem: it wasn't them, it was me.

Because here's the thing I've learned after interviewing over 1500 men: no man thinks about committing. Sure, there are some crazy fellas who decide that the minute they meet you, they want to put a ring on it. But these blokes are few and far between. And if that's your bloke, you probably wouldn't be reading this book. So read on . . .

Men are not built like we are. There is no biological clock ticking along for them. In fact, the longer they remain single, the more of a Catch they become. Yes, that's right. Women hit 30 and already they worry they'll never find someone to settle down with. Men hit 30, and they suddenly discover that the world is their oyster! Why commit when they have the gamut of the dating pool at their fingertips? The younger women are falling at their feet; the older ones are looking for a toy boy who knows what he's doing. And his mates are telling him that if he ever dares to get married, it will be the end of his single life (and his sex life) as he knows it.

But don't be disheartened just yet. At a wedding the other day, a groom—who was a notorious playboy and told anyone who listened that he'd only ever get married after he turned 35—was sitting at the bridal table with his new wife at a measly 29. So what made him do it? What made him commit?

Firstly, he had to chase his bride to be. She just wasn't interested. Secondly, she supported him when he was at his lowest point. He didn't have a job and had difficulty finding work during the GFC. And when men feel like they don't have a career to call their own, they feel like less of a man and in turn feel like they can't be the man a woman wants them to be.

So here's the catch: sometimes you are ensconced in a relationship that is *realistically* going to go nowhere. Now, I don't want to be the bearer of bad news here, but your boyfriend right this minute might actually *never* commit to you, no matter how many tactics you employ or how much you beg and cajole or how many games you play or blow jobs you give.

And if you want commitment, make sure you're not dating any of the following types either:

- The guy who says he's sort of seeing someone else but not at the moment.
- The guy who wants to go and live overseas.
- The guy who is still studying.
- The guy who has just come out of a long-term relationship.
- The guy who still lives at home with his mum.

The word 'exclusive'

A man told me that he decided he was going to commit to his girlfriend the day (after three months of being casual) she asked him if they were exclusive. 'Or should I start dating other people too?'

He also told me this: 'If a girl said, "I want to be married within a year", I'd break up with her. Committing and marriage still needed to be my decision. I might be a lovely guy—I'm still the man. I don't have a timeline. In a perfect world, get married, have kids. I've already had a long-term relationship for over two years now—I'm not in a rush.'

Don't be afraid to lose him

The key to really getting a man to commit is being unafraid to lose him. After six months of dating a man she was truly in love with, Sharon came to the day when she decided that enough was enough. He hadn't spoken about the future to her at all, and so she gave herself an ultimatum: 'If he doesn't speak to me about the future within the next month, I'm going to start dating other people.'

She had already brought it up with him in a subtle way. She'd asked him where he thought things were going and he said he wasn't sure.

#45.   THE INNER ULTIMATUM

This is your most powerful tool when wanting to get a man to commit to you. If he doesn't respond to your subtle request, give yourself your own timeline and, when the deadline passes, feel free to pull away and start dating other people. The key is being unafraid to lose him. And then you'll see his monogamous gene kick in.

When the next month rolled on, she pulled right back. She stopped answering all his calls, she made plans with other people when they were supposed to have a date night and she generally acted a little less interested than she had previously.

And guess what? Her man stepped it right up. He called her up and asked her if she would like to accompany him to look at rings. She was elated!

Of course, she didn't want to lose him at all. But if he wasn't going to step it up and commit to her soon, she was going to have to be prepared to do so. Because that's how Catches behave. They don't wait around for all eternity for a man to commit to them—they know there are hundreds of other men just around the corner who will.

I, on the other hand, was always afraid of losing the men I was dating. In fact, I thought every single man I met during my crazy dating year was 'the one'. But how wrong I was. In fact the more I dated, the more I realised that every subsequent guy I would be with was a better Catch than the last!

The second guy came into my life literally two days after I ended it with the first. From *no effort* on my part other than attending every social function I was invited to. What an improvement! By the time the third guy rolled around, I couldn't even believe I'd called the last two guys Catches! And so it continued—each man I met would be better than the previous one.

But at the time, when I met a man—any man—I'd tell all my friends that I'd finally met someone who was 'the one'—he was *it*! I was so impressed at myself for meeting him and so proud to finally be able to gloat to all my friends that I had a boyfriend that I'd quickly tell everyone I could about it. I hated the stigma of being single and so when I got a man in my life (usually after a few dates) I'd shout it from the rooftops to anyone who would listen that I, Sam Brett, was *no longer single*!

Well, you can imagine what happened next. It wasn't the fact that I was in love with the guy, but it was the sheer embarrassment of possibly losing him that killed me. I'd feel that if I didn't hear from him or see him every other day that I would be a failure. That I'd be single again. That everyone would be looking at me and thinking that I was a complete and utter loser and that I wasn't worthy enough for a boyfriend.

And then the minute I'd meet the next man, I'd do the *exact same thing*. And then it just got to a point where people no longer took me seriously.

'Oh, that's just another one of Sam's romantic stories that will last two weeks and then it will all be over.' And stories there were ... in abundance. Until one day, I was hanging out in Thailand with my perennially single (older) girlfriend over the New Year break and she turned to me and said, 'Babe, there's nothing so great about being in a relationship anyway. Do you really want to be stuck on the couch for the rest of your life? Because once you're in it, there's no turning around and getting back this life.'

I took a look at where we were—on the beach of Phi Phi, a stone's throw from the hottest clubs in the world where the booze flowed freely, freer than the breasts of the topless women waltzing past, and I thought, yes, she's right. What if there was none of this ever again? What if this was the last time I was free to do what the heck I pleased, when I wanted to do it, and with whoever I wanted?

Would I really want to be clinging on to some guy I hardly knew in fear I'd never meet anyone else?

Sure, single life gets tiresome, boring and a little bit lonely at times. But you need to max it out for all it's worth. Find people who are at the same life stage as you and who want to take the world by the horns and ride it for all it's worth.

So if you want commitment, remember not to demand it instantly, but after a significant time has passed—around three to six months—give yourself an ultimatum. Make sure he's worth waiting around for, or move on!

A Cautionary Tale: Amanda

The night following J.J.'s blow-up at the launch for Amanda's collection, Amanda's best friend Tom flew in from New York. They'd been to school together and had always been best friends, from the day they met in Year Seven and sat next to each other in French class. J.J. was away and so she raced out the door to have dinner with Tom. She was oddly excited . . . something she hadn't felt around J.J. for a long time.

When she arrived at the restaurant Tom had picked (by the beach, low couches, low lighting, delectable cocktails), she was surprised to find him looking a little older, more professional and just as good-looking as she remembered. Amanda hadn't seen him in about a year, ever since he'd stopped making regular trips back home and had set up permanent camp in New York. A top attorney, he was making big waves over there. But when he was around her, he was just good old reliable Tom—the guy she'd cried to whenever she'd had a boy problem; who'd helped her with her maths homework in high school; who'd rescued her when she'd gotten sick after the first (and last) time she'd smoked pot.

'Wow, you look amazing,' he said as soon as he laid eyes on her, taking in her tight, black, cut-out Leona Edmiston dress.

'If that's your attempt at picking me up, it's not working,' she joked, nudging him in the ribs. She knew he'd always had

a crush on her but she was too busy dating older boys and then subsequently climbing the social ladder to notice him properly. Besides, he was one of her best friends—she'd never really even thought of him that way. He'd seen her at her worst, and he'd still always loved her.

She couldn't believe how comfortable it all was. Over dinner she asked him about his life in New York and he told her about all the crazy politics and superficiality that infiltrated the entire city.

They laughed and reminisced throughout dinner, and when she said something stupid about not knowing if Hong Kong was in China or not, he grabbed her hand, looked deeply into her eyes and said, 'Despite some people thinking you're a dumb blonde, I'm still your biggest fan. Even though you're now a redhead.'

She laughed. 'Definitely the worst pick-up line I've ever heard.'

After dinner, she didn't want their conversation to end. And it seemed neither did he. It was just all so natural. So . . . easy. They stopped on the way home to get a bottle of Café Patrón, and then they'd sat on her couch drinking it all night. Just like old times. Just like they used to be. Best friends who could tell each other anything. And he was as gorgeous as ever, in his grey T-shirt and jeans.

She sat opposite him on the couch, her legs curled underneath her, thinking how comfortable she felt around him. She'd definitely felt a strange tingle that she hadn't experienced with him before when he called to say he was in town. Maybe it was because he was the total opposite of J.J.—someone familiar, always loving towards her, always accepting of her—that she realised it was what she was craving. And tonight, something strange seemed to be in the air.

'Mandy, you look amazing in that dress,' he said softly.

'Thanks.' She giggled. 'I tried. Can't be an old married woman just yet.'

'Mand . . .' He paused, looking at her intently. 'I want to kiss you.'

Her heart skipped a beat as he moved closer to her on the couch. And then just as he leaned in, and right before he kissed her, he said, 'I've been waiting nearly twenty years for this.'

The following day, when J.J. returned home, he was in his usual foul mood. 'There's fake tan on the sheets,' he barked. 'And this place is a fucking pigsty. I can't live like this any more.'

Amanda took a deep breath in. She wasn't quite sure where she was going with this, but she did know that getting married to him was not the right decision. And that, somehow, this was one decision she was not going to regret.

Months of fighting had led to this; him chipping away at her self-esteem, at her soul and, finally, at her love.

'I'm giving you the ring back,' she said quietly, slowly removing her diamond.

He turned around, darting a confused look in her direction.

'You're what?' he replied, disbelievingly.

Silence. A single tear rolled down her cheek. She glanced up at him, wondering if he was going to fight for her. But all she saw was a smug grin forming on his face.

'*You think you'd ever get any better than me? Ha! You're a joke, Amanda. You're old. Damaged goods.*'

When she didn't reply (she had no strength to fight back at him), he said, 'Fine. Do what you want. I'm calling my parents.'

She went into the bedroom, picked up her emergency leave bag and put on her shoes. She was finally doing this. She was getting out. She felt like everything was going in slow motion. It all felt so wrong, yet so right at the same time. How could that be? Was she making the biggest mistake of her life?

She didn't know where she was going, or if she'd ever find someone again. What she did know was that Tom had inspired something deep inside of her, some deep-rooted knowing that the type of man she wanted to be with was not the one standing in the other room, gloating to his parents that he was finally free of 'all this wedding bullshit'.

She loved J.J. deeply—hell, he'd fought hard to win her. He'd even proposed—in his romantic way—after six months! And now she was tossing it all away. For what? She didn't exactly know. But she realised this life—the life they'd built together—wasn't the life she wanted to live any longer.

And with that she walked out the front door . . .

14

The Girlfriend Catch: Three + months

So you're his girlfriend, now what?

My friend Stacey—who is in a long-term relationship with a younger man—is the ultimate Girlfriend Catch. Why? Because she has her man eating out of the palm of her hand three years on . . . and things are still going strong. Stacey knows exactly how to be a girlfriend that a man adores. So let's look at what The Catch does to keep him there.

She isn't always available

The Catch is extremely busy with her career, her social life and her exercise regime. And so she isn't available every single time her man contacts her. Sometimes she doesn't answer his calls or doesn't call him back. And he always calls again. Sure, when you're in a long-term relationship you're not supposed to play games or make a man chase. But when you're dating a dude who seems to be in demand with a gaggle of other women often surrounding him, you need to ensure that you are constantly projecting that you are the ultimate Catch material. Keeping him on his toes through occasionally not being contactable is the first step to doing this. A man likes to feel he's doing the chasing and he will never get complacent with you if you still make him feel like he doesn't quite 'have' you—at least not until he proposes!

She looks super hot at all times

When you become a girlfriend, you still need to dress exactly like you would as the Single Catch. After all, your man worked very hard to chase you—surely he should be rewarded for his efforts?

Girlfriend Catches are extremely aware of the fact that their man bathes in the glory of knowing he caught the ultimate Catch. And therefore she strives to let him know that indeed he did—every single day.

Whenever The Catch has a dinner date with her boyfriend, she makes sure her hair is clean and blow-dried, her nails aren't chipped but rather are freshly painted, her make-up is applied immaculately and her clothes are clean, ironed, sexy and sophisticated. She wants to ensure that her boyfriend continues to see her as a Catch, and that neither of them become complacent or bored in the relationship.

There is much to be learned from the way the Girlfriend Catch tackles her relationship in regards to her appearance. Her boyfriend is still smitten with her—many years on. He sees himself as the luckiest guy on the planet every time he looks at her. Sure, they have movie nights where they stay in and she wears her favourite trackies and has her hair in a bun. But that is saved for those special occasions when they decide to be chilled-out together. This isn't an everyday occurrence. When he comes home from work, she is always freshly showered and wearing something gorgeous, and not too expensive either.

#46. THE GIRLFRIEND CATCH

The Girlfriend Catch never gets complacent with her looks or her grooming. She does it as much for her man as she does for herself. Because the way you look is the way you feel, and a great girlfriend looks and feels like a million dollars!

The same goes for newlyweds, new mums and wives. The longer you're in a relationship, the better you should look. Don't give up just because you've nabbed your man. And you don't have to do it solely for him either. Do it for yourself. Because confidence in yourself breeds confidence in the relationship. And when you're happy, he's happy and everyone gets along swimmingly. Keep things sexy, alive and going smoothly by putting in that extra bit of effort. You'll be thankful later on.

Girlfriend Catches are also killer cooks. They make meals that their man can then go and brag to his mates about.

How to get a man to propose in *six* steps

We've all experienced the moment when we discover that we're suddenly not getting any younger. And yet the prospect of marriage is not any closer either. After all, there might not even be a man in the picture! Or if there is, he's not really doing anything about proposing. He either hasn't mentioned the 'M' word, or if he has, he seems to be stalling. And yet here you are, starting to get more and more desperate by the nanosecond. All your friends are getting hitched! When is your turn for god's sake?

Even if you don't have a man yet, you might find yourself starting to look (rather seriously) at wedding dresses. You get weak in the knees when you walk past a jewellery store. You've decided on your venue. Which is all fine and good, as long as you *keep it to yourself*.

But when marriage is on your mind, and you start to freak out every man you meet by mentioning it before you've managed to finish your first cocktail on a first date, you're not going to get closer to the altar—you're going to freak him the heck out.

I'm sick to death of listening to women who, while they are desperate to get married, have no idea how to go about doing it. They are too afraid to say anything to their man so instead they're stuck on a merry-go-round of bad relationships, never stopping to ask the dude in question what he wants . . . and if indeed marriage is on the cards. Then there are those women who mention their desire for marriage on every first date, scaring the bloke in the entirely different direction! The good news is that there are indeed two types of men: the ones who want to make a woman happy and commit, to provide and protect her for the long term. And then there are those men stuck in player mode for whom marriage is the furthest thing from their minds.

From the Male Room

'Proposing takes time and when the timing is right, that's only when you'll find guys will do it. Being financially stable I think is the key. That's how guys think: when we have all our ducks in a row and we're happy and stable in our job and career, that's when we'll be more likely to propose.'—**Jamie**

'I was desperate to propose to my girlfriend, especially since we didn't live together. I have lived with other girlfriends in the past and it did not work.'—**Steve**

Six-Step Marry-Me Plan

Step 1: Pick the right guy

Yep, you heard it here first: there's no point in getting married unless you're with the right guy. I know this sounds like the easiest part.

'But I already have a man!' you might be thinking. Well, good for you. But there are important things that you need to consider and you need to be entirely honest with yourself about them. Because here's the thing: love, commitment and stability are not reasons to get married. Compatibility is. And when we are ensconced in a heady relationship of lust and sex, sometimes we put aside this very small point.

Also, we are no longer in the position our mothers found themselves in. We're financially independent, strong women who are so used to being single we no longer actually rely on a man as much. Of course it's rather nice to have a bloke by your side. In fact, there's nothing I like more than some good male company. But the reasons women got married in the past—financial stability, to create a family, have security and a future—those reasons no longer apply. So you might as well be a little more savvy about what man you pick to spend the rest of your life with . . . till death do you part. And that means there are a certain number of things you shouldn't put up with, namely, abuse of any sort; cheating, lying, untrustworthiness; or any red flags that might pop up during your time of courtship.

#47.   DON'T MARRY A JERK

Before you work out how to get a man to propose, make sure he is the right guy. Marriage is a huge decision—don't take it lightly just because you want a sparkling new ring.

And if you find yourself one of those women who is in a relationship with a man you're desperately wanting to get married to, but you can't quite understand why he won't propose already, here are some reasons why he might not be taking the plunge with you.

He doesn't feel like he's in a financially stable enough position to get married

When a masculine, sensitive, real man decides to get married, he also decides to take on the financial responsibility to provide for you and your future family. Real men know that if they're not yet in a position to do so, they don't want to put a ring on it until they are. So he strives to do everything in his power to get there.

But here's the other big *but*: if this sounds like your man, and he's not taking the steps to become financially stable, but instead prefers to party, drink beers with his buddies and live in a frat house, then you're going to be waiting a very long time. So then you have to weigh up the pros and cons: Is he really worth you waiting around for him? Are there literally no other men in the world? Is this the last man on the planet who will ever give you a chance at true happiness?

He's a Stringer

When a man doesn't truly want to commit, but nevertheless decides to date you with a different goal to you in mind, he is a bona fide Stringer. The problem with dating a Stringer is that because they're so good at being perfect boyfriend material, you fall in love with them. And eventually, because they can never give you what you want, you get burnt. (See Chapter 8.)

Reasons he's the wrong man for you

He's abusive

Physical abuse is not tolerated. End of story. I don't care how much you love him. The truth is he's never going to change. And this is the *rest of your life*.

Emotional abuse, on the other hand, is something that a lot more women tolerate. Your man puts you down, tells you you're worthless or insults you one too many times. You fight, you make up and you think he'll stop. But alas, he does it again. And again.

Before you know it, your self-esteem, self-worth and *self* go out the window. You no longer have confidence in your decisions, your life, yourself. You spiral further and further down into a funk. You become dependent on him. And that's exactly his aim. He never wants you to leave. And he's winning. The more you let it go on, the more you lose yourself and the harder it is to get out.

Please, do yourself a favour, and never, ever let things get to this point. Because it takes a lot of strength to get out of it. Strength which he will have made sure he's sucked right out of you. You don't deserve that life. But if you have a pattern of choosing these sorts of men—and many women do, which sometimes stems from the way they were treated during childhood— then you need to break it. And it's easier said than done. Unfortunately the only thing that is going to break the abuse cycle is therapy. Get some.

He's a liar/cheater

Really? You *really* want to marry this cad? Wake up and smell the male pheromones! Men like this don't change. And you can only imagine how much worse it's going to get when you have kids . . . Unfortunately, no matter how charming a man might seem, there are some men out there who are simply professional charmers, players and geniuses at roping women in under false pretences. Sure, he says he'll change, but really, do you want to be constantly worrying about your security? I think not.

He has an addiction

A man who has an addiction such as drugs, alcohol or sex and is in denial or isn't dealing with it through constructive or professional help is very bad news. His problems will become your problems. Your love—and marriage—cannot fix him. Your good days will depend on him not 'using'.

He's a Womaniser

A womaniser is a man that is never satisfied with just one woman, but likes to gather a harem, even if only in thought. He's the type who thinks it's OK to stare women up and down while he's with you and is constantly thinking and talking about women, not just you. He may accuse you of being jealous or oversensitive, when the reality is . . . he's the one with a problem. He has no respect for you and his wandering eye won't be cured with marriage.

He's emotionally unavailable

This will eventually drain you. You'll soon long for someone who is emotionally available and able to give in the way you need. If you marry an emotionally unavailable man, you'll have an emptiness that he will not be able to fill.

He's a moocher

He's lazy and finds excuses not to work, but has no problem mooching off your hard-earned income. He may be charming, but you'll soon catch on that he's in the marriage for his benefit and you aren't getting much out of it. You give and he continues to take.

There are always exceptions to the rules, but observe closely the type of man you are considering marrying. The right partner will enhance your life, not make you have deep regrets for being with them. To quote Robert C. Dodds: 'The goal in marriage is not to think alike, but to think together.'

If you pick a drug addict, a player or someone who isn't right for you, you are going to end up divorced, separated or unhappy.

Just want to get married so you're with anyone? No—you need to marry your best friend because you will be with them for the rest of your life.

Marriage is an extremely important decision. In fact, it's going to be the biggest business decision of your life. Many people overlook this little factoid. But the fact is your whole life is ahead of you and the partnership you choose now is the partnership you're going to choose forever.

So you need to take into account whether they're your best friend, whether you're sexually compatible and whether your lifestyles match one another's.

Once you've got the right one—on paper and in real life—then you've got something to work with.

Step 2: Date him

- Yes, date him. Casually, seriously, whatever you want. Just don't mention anything about marriage, the future or settling down for at least the *first three months*.

- Always be sexy, be flirty and be hot! Once you're dating him, this isn't the time to let your guard down. Remember what we spoke about in terms of the Girlfriend Catch? Be that Catch throughout your courtship (and your life!).

- Work out what your man's needs and wants are and then provide them. Constantly ask questions about his likes and dislikes. Learn what turns him on and what turns him off. And make sure he's giving you what you want in return. But also remember: men aren't mind readers either. So don't be afraid to let him know (subtly) what you like and what you don't.

From the Male Room

'Too many women think men are mind readers. And so they go through a relationship being unhappy, when in fact all they needed to do was open their mouths and articulate what they need! Never do it in a nagging way either. Always say it gently and warmly. Men want to please you—so let us!'—**Ben**

- Let him fall in love with you: That's right—let him fall in love with you. And the way you do that? Continue with your Catch exercises. Continue to look after yourself, run fast, be well groomed— whatever it takes to make you feel like the ultimate Catch at all times.

Emotional attraction: How a man stays in love

Emotional attraction is the thing that gets a man to open up, to share his feelings and connect with a woman on a deeper level than he usually allows into his life. It's what bonds a man to one woman over the long term.

When a man says that he doesn't feel 'in love' with you any more, what he's really saying is: 'I used to feel both physical and emotional attraction with you. But the way our relationship has been, I'm not feeling much, if any, of that emotional attraction now. And because of that, what I feel in my heart and my head tells me that something is "off" in our relationship, and I don't know what to do about it.'

What he needs to feel it again

When a man asks for or creates distance or space, it's tempting to try to resist it and grab on tighter—but that only backfires. That's because people naturally tend to want to run away from something that is running to them. He'll feel like you're forcing closeness, and he'll want out of it.

Instead, you want to create emotional attraction between the two of you in order to reconnect. Here's how.

1. Allow him the space he needs and take some space for yourself

That means you take all that energy and attention you've been putting into holding the relationship together and instead redirect it towards your own life: your friends; your hobbies; whatever makes you happy.

When you do this, something magical happens. First, you feel empowered over the situation so that your emotions do not overtake you. Second, men often move past their own doubts and fears in their own time when given space (a few hours or days) to do so.

2. Shake things up a little to create interest and excitement for both of you

Remember what I said before about attraction and love happening for a man because of newness and unpredictability?

Well, if a close, connected relationship with your man has fizzled out, you can jump-start things by introducing new and unpredictable ways of relating to him.

So, if you normally have the same weekend routine, mix it up. Come up with something different and interesting to do. Pick a sport that you can do with him; go out and meet new people together; explore different ways to be intimate together; plan a trip somewhere you've always wanted to go to. And if you are together all the time, spending time apart as in point one creates newness and unpredictability, too.

If things are stalling in your relationship with a man but you used to feel very connected to him, this is actually good news for you. That's because you already have all the ingredients you need to relight the fire of the relationship. If he was physically and emotionally attracted to you before, you can inspire the same level of closeness again. All it takes is keeping the emotional attraction strong by giving him the space he needs and creating fresh opportunities to keep you both excited about your time together.

Don't mention marriage in the beginning. This is the time for you to concentrate on falling in love, sharing cocktails, immersing yourselves in each other's lives and having fun. Stretch out the honeymoon period for as long as possible!

#48.   GET HIM TO FALL IN LOVE WITH YOU

The Catch allows a man the space to fall in love with her without badgering him into it. She knows how to incite a strong, deep, emotional connection without letting him ever feel like he was duped into it.

Step 3: Get serious

Depending on your age and the speed at which your relationship is moving, you need to gauge when the best time is to get serious. I'd say that if you are seeing each other most days, and he's showing you some serious signs that he's into you and that he's ready for a commitment, then you can start this step at around four months. If you aren't seeing each other that often, and things are very casual between the two of you, you may want to speed things up after the four-month mark with your *actions*. (Remember, men deal with things through actions, not words.) And then you can start doing the 'get serious' phase after six months. But six months should be your mental deadline. After all, you are not the type of girl who is going to be waiting around forever for some guy to start wanting to commit to you. You have better things to do!

If, however, you are one of those speedy couples, then let's start talking about what's going to happen at the four-month mark. You are going to start thinking about commitment and possibly marriage. *He is not.* Remember that. So the key is to start planting the seeds at this point. Be very careful not to jump the gun here, and also be wary of your words. And of not becoming too clingy either. I know there are a lot of rules, but men are such different creatures from us: they have no biological clock and, worst of all, the more they age, the more options they have available to them! That's why it's so important that for four whole months, you work on making him fall in love with you. That way he has more to lose by losing you.

Step 4: The four (or six) month mark

Congratulations! You've made it. You've dated and made him fall in love with you and you've survived the hardest part of the dating jungle: making him into your boyfriend. Now, before you jump in and start questioning whether or not he'll commit to you, this is where you take the power back. You need to step back and

---

#49. WAIT AT LEAST FOUR MONTHS BEFORE BRINGING UP COMMITMENT

Four months—and no sooner—is when you bring up commitment, if he hasn't already done so himself. But do it wisely, and then sit back and let him come up with his very own solution.

---

decide if he is indeed the one for you. Do you really want to be with this man for the long haul? Go back to step one and read the checklist. Ask yourself: Is he really the man for me? Is he looking at other skirts? Is he going to be a good provider? Is he showing you that he really cares? Then, and only then, are you allowed to ask him what he wants in regards to his future. You need to ascertain what his timeline is. And then you need to set your own.

Make sure you are not in the 'fun' zone either. If his response is that he's just having fun and that he is enjoying the way things are going and doesn't want to think about the future, it's still very important that you ask him if he ever wants to get married. Don't mention a thing about your own timeline. At this point you're just gauging his. We'll come to yours in a minute.

Step 5: Set yourself a timeline

If you want to get married in the next couple of years or next few months, and you find your man is not stepping up to the plate, it's time to pull back a little from him. Pouring yourself out to him on a platter doesn't make you The Catch. Because he's got nothing to chase any longer. Which is why it's imperative you don't move in with him until there's a ring on your finger. Instead of telling him that there's something you 'need to talk about'—which only makes *any* man pull back—rather, just do the opposite. *Show* him (don't tell him) that you're not waiting around until he is ready and that you have a fabulous life to live whether he's in it or not. The key here is to help him realise that he can't really live without you. *That is the key*.

Step 6: Have the conversation

All right girl, you've earned it. Once you've pulled back and he starts to ask you what's wrong and if you're having second thoughts about him, then you can say something. And only then.

Instead of saying 'I have something to talk about'— pull back.

When he asks you what's wrong or questions you, tell him this: 'I don't know if I want this to go any further, because in the next two years I see myself married or engaged. I'm having fun with you—sex is great, our friendship is great . . . and I love to muck around but I don't even know if we are right. I need to know before we go any further, is this something you see yourself wanting? Do you want the same things, or is there absolutely no way?'

Let him think about it. Then let him keep falling in love with you. At six (or eight) months, you can bring it up more seriously. He doesn't want to lose you because now he's invested way too much into this serious relationship to let that happen. And if you do this properly, then you are not reeking of desperation. You are simply saying, 'I like you but this is what I want. I'm falling in love and never intended to have serious emotions, and I need to let you know what I want.'

The marriage recap

So let's recap exactly what you've done here:

1. *You reel him in*—make him fall in love with you.
2. *Putting it out there*—after four months together you start planting the seed that you want something more. And this seed will start to grow and, if he loves you, grow in the right way.
3. *He's silently starting to work out how he's going to provide for and protect you*—at the stage when he is contemplating this, you don't have to do anything else but sit on the sidelines and continue to allow him to fall in love with you.
4. *Bring it up again*—around two months after you've planted the seed.

This is not to say that all men will marry you after this, but it is the best way to let him know what you want without scaring him off.

From the Male Room

'I never even thought about marriage. Men don't. But when I noticed that it was what was going to make my girlfriend happy, I decided, to heck with it! I wanted to make her happy. And if getting her a ring would make her happy, then that's exactly what I ended up doing. We've been married for three years and it was the best decision I ever made.'—**Jed**

A Cautionary Tale: Amanda

When Amanda Potts and J.J. Brentwood broke their engagement off, the media had a field day.

GOLDEN COUPLE SPLIT!

KEN DUMPS BARBIE!

But Amanda was determined not to let it get her down. She immediately called Tom in New York.

She told him the whole sordid tale. She cried and she cried some more. And then she stopped. There was silence.

'Can I talk now?' Tom asked.

'Shoot.'

'Listen to me. I love you, Mandy. I've loved you from the day I met you. Regardless of whether you're a supermodel or a little kid in maths class. You're my Achilles heel, my life, my "it". I've been searching for someone just like you to be with my whole life. And that doesn't make sense when I could just be with you.'

Amanda didn't know what to say. She knew she loved Tom dearly, but was she in love *with him?*

'Come see me in New York,' he was saying.

'I'll think about it.'

Amanda hung up the phone, poured herself a glass of wine and sank down onto her parents' couch with a sigh. Being back at home was a nightmare, but anything was better than her previous situation. And now Tom's offer was starting to play on her mind. Thoughts began to race in her head as she started to think about it. She was his 'one' and she knew that he would treat her like an absolute princess for the rest of her life. The more she thought about it, the better it all sounded. Yes, perhaps she was more in love with him than she first thought. And isn't that what she really wanted deep down? A man who actually loved her for her, without all the bells and whistles? Who knew her more intimately than anyone else, and who not only worshipped her, but had been her rock all those years?

Suddenly another thought occurred to her. She'd already conquered the fashion world pretty seamlessly on her own turf. What if . . . she could do the same in New York? What if she, Amanda Potts, could make it on her own, without a man propping her up, in the big city? The mere thought of her very own bikinis sitting on rails in New York city department stores made her stomach tickle from the adrenaline. The thought of pulling off this little subterfuge was exactly the type of challenge she was looking for. In fact, for the first time since the split, she actually began to get excited about something. Yes, she could do it. She would do it. After all, she already had contacts in all the right places. Surely it couldn't be that hard?

Amanda did fly to New York . . . And then she'd walked into Barneys and they'd ordered the entire range of her swimwear line. She couldn't believe what was happening to her. But she knew everything happened for a reason. As she walked hand in hand with Tom through Central Park, she looked back on her last year and sighed. Everything was perfect! How had this happened? People dream their entire lives about meeting their soul mate through some magical twist of fate. And yet hers had been right under her nose the entire time. She looked at Tom and smiled. She was deliriously, truly and utterly happy for the first time since she could remember . . .

A Cautionary Tale: Camilla

A month after moving into her new flat, Camilla was sitting on the blue futon next to Kade, watching Wheel of Fortune. *She had put the thought that he was the sexiest man alive worthy of a* People *magazine award right out of her head and now she was sitting in her favourite trackies with her legs crossed underneath her and her hair in a ponytail, talking to him like they were old friends. True to her word, Tracey was hardly ever there, and Kade and Camilla were starting to spend all their spare time together.*

Kade vanished for a few minutes, and then returned carrying two glasses of red wine. He was obsessed with wines, and he'd decided that he and Cam would try a new type each night.

'Hmm . . . a little fruity,' Kade said, swishing the wine around in his mouth.

'Fruity? I think it's more like full-bodied, a little spicy, and—what's that I taste? Cinnamon?' Camilla said sarcastically.

'After all this time with me, and you still know nothing about wines, do you?' Kade replied playfully. 'In fact, since you know so little, how about I take you to my favourite wine bar tonight and we do some real taste testing?'

Camilla's heart gave a little tug, but she ignored it. It was just her flatmate inviting her for a drink because they had nothing better to do. Nothing more—nothing less. Keep it together, *she told herself.*

'Sure.' She shrugged nonchalantly. 'I'll just change.'

'Wow, you don't sound too excited about it. Maybe I should leave you here and invite one of the boys?'

She punched him on the arm. 'Anything beats Wheel of Fortune. Even spending the evening with you.'

When they got to the wine bar, Camilla was in heaven. The place was dark, dingy and underground, and a jazz singer sat crooning in the corner. Candles dotted the room along with fresh flowers and there was a scent so delectable she wanted to stay forever. The next few hours were no different. Cam and Kade talked, drank wine, drank more wine, laughed and talked some more. As they stumbled out of the wine bar, they were both still laughing at something Camilla had said earlier.

'Wow, that was a lot of wine,' Camilla said, smiling at the warm fuzzy feeling that was enveloping her. Kade gazed at her and she saw something wistful in his eyes; something warm, loving and trustworthy. She also noticed he was gazing at her longer than usual. She knew she should turn away, but she didn't want to. Instead she looked directly back at him. He was moving towards her and suddenly their lips were touching. They fell into a taxi together, and didn't stop kissing all the way to their door.

15

Keeping him interested

Top tips for keeping a man interested

Men need variety

Advises Donna Sozio, my co-author for *The Man Whisperer*: 'To keep a wandering eye in check, and to keep him interested in you for the long term and always viewing you as The Catch, men need variety. He constantly needs new things: trips, exciting adventures, different sexual positions—whatever. You just can't get stuck in a routine. He can't see you in the same grey track pants every day. Women make the mistake of thinking that once they've got the guy, they're done and don't have to do anything any more to keep his interest. But a wedding ring isn't a prison sentence. He is free to leave. So if you want him to stay, you need to keep being the woman he fell in love with, even more so because seeing the same person every day can get mightily boring. Part of being The Catch is keeping up your interests and your physical appearance, keeping a good attitude, trying something new with your partner, all to keep his interest.'

Men need to feel like they're succeeding in the relationship and making their partner happy

Women should adopt a language technique that makes men feel they are succeeding in pleasing their partner. The more a man feels like he is succeeding in pleasing you, the more he will feel pleased with himself. Says Donna: 'It is important to never put your partner down and to always make him feel like his efforts are rewarded.'

My married friend Lana does this beautifully. She is constantly making sure that despite the fact she is one of the most capable, brilliant women I know, she always lets her man know if she is in distress and needs his help. 'Honey, I'm so stressed about x, do you think you might be able to help me/give me advice/save the day?'

Even if she is completely capable of doing it without his help, she still makes sure that she lets him know that he is needed. Men aren't like women; when women get asked to do things, we feel like we are not doing a good enough job. When men get asked to do things for us, they feel proud that they are needed and want to do a good job in order for us to be proud of them. The more we thank them, the more they want to do things for us. And the more we reward good behaviour, the more they want to continue with this good behaviour pattern.

A word on nagging

Do not confuse posing a polite request to your man with the thing that men abhor the most—nagging. In *The Man Whisperer*, Donna and I talk copiously about the fact that the fastest way to kill a relationship is with incessant nagging. There are other ways to ask a man to do something for you, and that often involves phrasing things in a way that doesn't sound like a demand, but rather advice or help or an opportunity to provide win-win situations. It is true that sometimes your man just won't seem to step it up . . .

The Catch doesn't stay in an overdue relationship

The courage it took Amanda to leave her relationship is incredible, and many girls aren't lucky enough to have the same strength. But when you are in an unhappy relationship, you need to seriously weigh up the pros and cons of being in the relationship, then really work out what you want.

It's not enough to say that you love him, there needs to be more: security, a foundation of respect, love and trust.

And then if you decide it all isn't for you, then you need to make the leap of faith—you don't know what's waiting for you on the other side. It's easy when you have something waiting in the wings but of course when you are starting from scratch, it can be extremely painful and it takes a lot of courage to walk away.

♥ #50.   THE CATCH AND INNER STRENGTH

The Catch finds a way to exit a relationship that is no longer working for her. She doesn't stay past its use-by date and she doesn't worry about disappointing those around her. She knows that she must do what is best for her at all times. And must never accept a man treating her badly.

Rachel, a 30-year-old publicist, was engaged to Stuart. And she was pregnant. He didn't want her to have the baby. In fact, there were a number of occasions where he seriously threatened her if she decided to go ahead with it. She knew it was his own issues and insecurities leading him to behave like this, but somehow the relationship no longer felt right for her.

She knew the embarrassment she would cause both their families should she cancel the wedding with only a few months to go. After all, she'd purchased her dress, booked the venue and everything had been paid for. But nevertheless she now knew in her heart that she'd made the entirely wrong decision. And she wasn't about to let it get in the way of the rest of her life. And so she did it—she left the relationship.

Rules for a broken engagement:

- Send a formal letter to everyone invited to the wedding two weeks after the break-up.
- Send back the engagement gifts.
- When people ask the reason, tell them that you love each other very much but you've decided to go in different directions.
- Stay away from gossip. People will love to talk about it all. Don't be a part of it. Give them absolutely nothing to feed off.

A Cautionary Tale: Camilla

'Camilla!' Nate said, spotting her at the other side of the restaurant.

'Hi!' Camilla said. She waved and walked towards him slowly (or rather, 'swanned' towards him), her bellini sloshing out of her glass. She licked her hand.

Camilla bent down and gave him a kiss on his cheek.

'Are you here with another guy?' he said. He looked her up and down and took in her hot pink minidress and toned, tanned limbs.

'Maybe I am, what's it to you?' Camilla smiled at him. No-one fucks with Camilla Mason any more.

'Nothing. It's just that I didn't want you to get upset when you met my girlfriend.'

'Oh, so you finally let her out of the cupboard? How lucky for her,' Camilla said.

'Nah, got rid of that one . . . She was just too needy. I'm here with—'

Out of the corner of her eye, Camilla saw a mass of black curls and sequins bounding towards them. The girl put her hands over Nate's eyes and kissed his neck. 'Guess who?' she said in an annoying voice.

Camilla felt a warm arm encircle her waist. She turned around and smiled when she saw Kade looking deeply into her eyes. His kind, gentle eyes gazing into hers.

'Hey, beautiful,' he whispered into her ear. 'Sorry to interrupt, man,' Kade said to Nate, 'but our dinner has arrived. I'm Kade, nice to meet you!'

He grabbed Camilla's hand and she squeezed it back. Camilla felt a warm fuzziness pervade her. She had Kade. She really did. A guy who knew what Diptyque perfume was, who complimented her French manicure when she messed it up—who told her she was beautiful when she was brushing her teeth and had pimple cream on her face. And the sex—oh my god . . . the sex . . . night after night they'd have mind-blowing orgasmic sex, which made her legs shake and her body ache and her insides crave for more.

There were two seats at their candlelit table but as Camilla stared at his gorgeous face, she couldn't help feeling like she wanted to be closer to him. Way closer. She plonked herself on his lap and gave him a long, delectable kiss on the mouth.

'Marry me,' he said as she stroked his bicep. God, it was huge—she still marvelled over it. Even after all these months. 'I love you, Milly. I want to be with you forever. I can't even imagine being apart from you for one night let alone years.'

Camilla felt tears springing to her eyes. Was she really going to do this? The thought of getting married had entered her head but she'd brushed it aside. After all, she had a life to live, a career to continue. Of course, she could always compromise. And she did seriously love those white dresses. She had finally found her perfect man, so what was so scary? Yes, marrying Kade would be good. Besides, what would she do without Kade by her side?

'Yes. OK,' Camilla said, smiling.

'Really? Are you being serious?'

'Dead serious.' She kissed him again.

'Well then, we'd better start going ring shopping!'

She giggled.

'Let's get out of here,' he whispered in her ear. 'I'll grab the bill and we'll get this to go.'

As Camilla waited outside the restaurant for Kade, she caught sight of Nate and the trashy-looking girl through the window. He was in the midst of animatedly telling her a story and she was giggling and gesturing at everything he said. Camilla could see his eyes narrowing as he paused and took a sip of his drink—a signal that nothing coming out of his mouth was sincere or real. It was all just part of his game . . . A game that she was no longer a part of at all, and never would be. A game that guys like Kade didn't play. She knew there was hope out there for her girlfriends and her. Finally, she knew in her heart that the good guys were indeed out there, if you stop looking at every man as a potential and start waiting for them to come to you. She knew that no woman had to ever settle for anything less than their soul mate because he seriously was just around the corner—if you had the right attitude and let him chase you. The chase gene is in all men—you just have to give them a chance to use it. And a chance to catch you—because in essence, if you just believe you're The Catch, you certainly will be.

Final word

What I've learned from being single

Whoever said being single was easy was either drunk, getting laid or lying. While many might recall that their single days were filled with booze-induced hook-ups, endless independence, indulgence, freedom and more booze, they will still tell you that there were times when it just wasn't all as fun, exciting and filled with hot, satiating sex as many make it out to be.

Over the past year I've listened to the stories of others (often shocking, sometimes nasty and always riveting), asked questions, spoken to the experts and learned a heck of a lot about life, love and everything in between.

And I've had my own fair share of ups and downs. And god, have there been downs. I call it the 'crazy year'. From the moment I entered my break-up, to the moment I found 'the one' (which we'll get to in a minute), life was a roller-coaster ride of things that I never even fathomed were possible. You'll go through it all too—every single motion, every single type of man, every single type of emotion. There is no getting around the crazy year. When you're in it, you are willing it to end. You think you can't take any more of it. But when you finally get to the end of it, you look back and think that every single experience you had during the crazy year was worth the wait. Because you really do meet your prince. But only when you really and truly are ready. He will not show himself to you one nanosecond before then. Because if he did, you'd miss him.

My prince showed up to me in the form of my best friend from high school. It was like a fairytale. But he only showed up when I was completely and utterly 100 per cent ready for him to enter my crazy world. I finally had myself together. I was OK with being alone. I stayed home by myself for weeks on end, read books, did some writing and some major self-introspection. The best part about it was that we were already in love. There were no games. All the hard work had already been done during fifteen years of friendship. He lives on the other side of the world. But that doesn't matter. We will make it work. He is my soul mate.

When women like Meg would tell me that she'd found 'the one', I didn't believe her. But after I found my own one, I suddenly realised that it is indeed possible, if you are willing to put the work into yourself and make it happen—without going crazy.

So for those of you who are newly single, ready for a new relationship or just want to poke fun at the rest of the 4.7 million-odd lonesome souls who just can't seem to find a break, here are the mistakes, lessons and facts I've learned on the way. Don't say I didn't warn you!

Take at least three months to get to know someone before deciding whether you're in love with him

When you meet someone new who ticks most of your boxes, it's pretty easy to decide instantly that he could be 'the one'. Finally, after months (or years) you've met someone. Hooray! So you put all your eggs into this potentially good basket. You spend weeks (even months) putting huge amounts of effort into your new squeeze, without ever stopping to think that you should actually be getting to know the person, rather than just jumping blindly into a relationship because he meets all the criteria on some sort of checklist. Because as the weeks (or months) wear on and you suddenly find out a few unsavoury things about him, he might not be so appealing after all. But, wait, you're in love! You thought he was 'the one'! You told all your friends! So now what? Pain, hurt, embarrassment and thoughts of 'I'll never meet anyone' racing through your mind. And then you find yourself back at square one: alone and desperately looking for love and thinking you've found it in less than the time it takes to eat dessert together just because you want it so darn badly.

Don't think you can stay emotionally detached from your bonk buddy

When you're a sexually starved singleton, the knowledge that most men are up for it most of the time means that it's pretty easy to get laid. So you do. And then you realise that the bloke you've just bonked is up for nothing more than a semi-regular horizontal hanky-panky session. You surmise that, since the sex isn't too bad, you might as well get lucky a few times a week or month, rather than sit alone eating takeaway for one. But, inevitably, something starts to happen: you slowly become emotionally attached to your bonk buddy. And then, before you know it, you're fully fledged in love, and he's just using you . . . for sex. It's not a good feeling when you finally tell him your thoughts only to have him brush you aside like yesterday's newspaper.

Never date a friend . . . at least until you're 100 per cent certain

When you suddenly become single, there's a weird urge to scroll through the Facebook profiles of old friends/ lovers/ones you let get away to ascertain if any are newly single, if you might click with an old flame again or simply to bide some time. So you make an arrangement to catch up with one who responds to see if it could work, and you're mighty glad if it does. You end up making out and then inevitably regretting it the next day. The friendship will never be the same and all the reasons as to why it didn't work in the first place are conjured up. The solution? Don't go there. It's not worth the risk, the shame and losing the other half of your social crowd.

Find yourself a group of single friends but set the ground rules first

You're suddenly alone and you're ecstatic that you've found a bunch of mates to accompany you on your single girl expeditions. You love to talk about everything from boys to bonking, and relish the fact you've got something to do every Saturday night with people who aren't talking about babies, buying frying pans or taking out joint mortgages. But when two of you in the group suddenly become interested in the same target, or you find yourself on a date with one of their ex-flings, things can become a tad tricky. Suddenly things aren't so hunky-dory any more and jealousy, bitchiness and girl-on-girl fights (or boxing matches) ensue. The way around it? Set up the boundaries beforehand. Find out which people they have an absolute don't-go-there rule on, and then—quite simply—don't go there. Oh, and if you're out together and someone you're interested in is clearly into them, let them go with it. Tell them that they should do the same for you, and no-one will get hurt. We hope.

Ditch people with toxic energy

Without a partner to go home to, many tend to attract someone who majorly clings to them. Yet without an escape route, the last thing you need is toxic energy from toxic people coming into your life to bring your spirits down and take up all your spare time. Rid yourself of the people in your world who don't offer you any value but who instead try to suck the life and energy out of you. You're going to need all your energy for yourself if you're going to be fully equipped to deal with the treacherous dating jungle without negative influences in your life.

Ditch the games

I know, I know . . . this is a tough one. But with all the rules, games and confusing dating norms around, there's no doubt you're perplexed by what to do, when to do it, who pays, when to have sex, when to deflect their advances, when to play hard to get, when to put in the effort and when to let your guard down. Phew. And that's only in the beginning! If there's one thing I've learned, it's that, while there are no hard and fast rules, sometimes women tend to do something that ensures they put their foot in it no matter how into them the guy may be at first—like fantasy jumping. Don't get ahead of yourself, get to know him first and then any action you take with that in mind will reflect the fact you're just getting to know him. If he doesn't like you because you call or text too many times, he's not the right person for you anyway. Mature daters don't need games to spark sexual attraction. Or so we hope.

Women have got to smarten up

Always find yourself sitting at home waiting for his text message, regretting jumping into bed with him too soon, complaining there are no decent men in this town and always getting dumped? You've got to smarten up. And by that, I mean toughen up. There's the cliché that you've got to kiss a lot of frogs in order to find your prince and, with that in mind, it makes things not seem so bad after all. Everyone goes through it, everyone experiences the same caddish treatment, but remember: what you put out there is what you get back. Don't be that girl.

Don't let your biological clock cloud your judgement

The biggest topic of contention that has come up in recent discussions has been the loud ticking of the female biological clock. Men understand it's there, but they don't want to be told about it too early on in the union either (if at all). They know that many women want them to commit as soon as possible, but you need to know that men fear compromising their freedom, sex life and lifestyle any time soon, if ever. Of course there are those dudes who are mature enough to realise it might soon be time to settle down, but most are scared off by a woman mentioning anything of the sort.

'It should happen naturally!' he'll say, and then avoid the topic for as long as the woman will let him. Hence the trick is to get him thinking about it when the time is right, but not to put pressure on him either.

Forget social norms

Religion, age, life stage and a whole lot of other confusing factors play a big role in making a relationship work. But when you find someone you feel is worth sticking around for, you might want to put your prejudices aside. If you fear others will judge you, remember that they aren't the ones who have to live your life—you are.

Don't be jealous of your hitched-up friends

They don't have it so easy all the time either. But it's actually healthy to be around loved-up couples as often as possible (even if it makes you gag) as it puts everything into perspective, gives you hope that real love is indeed out there, and also enables you to see first-hand that relationships aren't always smooth sailing. Plus, they'll probably tell you to enjoy your single life for as long as bloody possible, which makes all these confusing rules, regulations and bad experiences seem not so bad after all.

Congratulations! You have made it through! You have survived being single, you have become The Catch and now you are ready and armed to meet the man of your dreams, if you haven't already.

Just remember at all times: You are The Ultimate Catch, and don't let anyone tell you otherwise.

Happy dating!!

Sam x

Epilogue

Meg moved to Canada, taking with her just one suitcase (mostly filled with her La Perla lingerie). She immediately got a job working for a female boss and soon after, Mark proposed in New York. Amanda and Tom were there to join in the toast as the four of them dined at Cipriani for the celebrations. As Meg sat looking dreamily over at her new fiancé, she realised that she had actually never experienced such loyal, kind treatment from a man before and realised she wanted to strive to do everything in her power to keep him happy. Plus, with her career back on track, she had big ambitions. She no longer craved the attention of random men (What a waste of time! she thought). Luckily Mark filled every one of her desires. And as Canada's new power couple, the two of them together had big plans.

Meanwhile at Cipriani, Tom had been planning his very own proposal to his one true love, Amanda. The minute

Meg and Mark had left the restaurant, Tom walked Amanda down to Times Square where he had an entire billboard lit up with the words, 'Marry Me Amanda'. Must have cost a fortune. The story ended up on the news and the sales of Amanda's bikinis skyrocketed. Everyone wanted a piece of the glamorous designer's romantic life, especially if that meant they could dress just like her for the imminent American summer. When J.J. caught wind of the story on the internet, he punched a mirror and ended up in hospital. His new girlfriend Pippa, a 19-year-old aspiring model, helped him make all the headlines once again. He claimed it was the result of a fall. Pippa, bathing in the glory, instantly launched her career as a television presenter for a travel show and promptly dumped J.J. He is currently enrolled in anger management classes.

Kate and Joey are still happily dating and Kate is rather thankful that her young boyfriend isn't the marrying type. She's decided that a big white wedding isn't for her anyway, and that living in the moment with a man who makes her feel ten times younger isn't such a bad thing after all. She has yet to discover if he has a Bad Boy side, but continues to periodically check his phone and emails for any suspicious behaviour, just in case.

The entire group flew to Sydney for Camilla's wedding to Kade, which took place on the Opera House steps with a glittering backdrop of the sunset on an idyllic night in the middle of summer. Fireworks and pistachio gelato ended the perfect evening before the four girls snuck away for a quiet moment in the corner.

'Here's to love,' Kate said, as the four girls clinked together their champagne glasses. Who knew . . .

Acknowledgments

What a team! Firstly I'd love to thank my incredible publisher, Louise Thurtell from Allen & Unwin, the best publisher a girl could ask for. Your unwavering support for me is so greatly appreciated, you'll never know. Thank you for giving the women of Australia the opportunity to hear from me time and time again.

To the rest of the brilliant Allen & Unwin team: firstly to Jo Lyons for an amazing editing job and for overseeing the entire book—what a task! To my copy-editor, Kylie Mason, and proofreader, Susin Chow, thank you for wading through my book and still wanting to speak to me afterwards.

To my agent, Jane Weston from Chic Celebrity, for believing in this project and for enjoying my dating tales almost as much as I enjoy living them.

To my beautiful, supportive, sensational, gorgeous girlfriends, Katrina, Monique, Justine, Jaime, Leigh, Donna and Hollie: you are the best examples of how the Ultimate Catch should look and behave. Your guidance, hilarious tales and endless support cannot be described in words. (And I'm supposed to be the wordsmith!)

To the men who have continued to give me fodder and fuel for this book, in order of appearance: Damien, Dave, Harry, Richie, Steve, Adam and all the men I interviewed, dated, dumped and was dumped by, thank you.

To Steve Jacobs from the *Sydney Morning Herald*, my subeditor in crime, what can I say? Your daily scrutiny of my writing has enabled me to look and sound smarter than I am. Thank you for putting up with me for all these years.

To my beautiful parents, Jon and Alice, and my awesome brother Dale, I love you all so much.

And finally, to all the readers of *Ask Sam* over the last six years, you guys are what drives my books and keeps me going day after day, reminding me of the importance of relationships, the perils of dating, and the magic of real, everlasting true love.

Sam xx

Endnotes

1. Scott Haltzman, *The Secrets of Happily Married Women*, Jossey-Bass, 2008.
2. Kristina Grish, *Addickted: 12 steps to kicking your bad boy habit*, Adams Media Corporation, 2006.
3. Louann Brizendine, *The Female Brain*, Broadway, 2006.
4. Steve Santagati, *The MANual: A true bad boy explains how men think, date, and mate—and what women can do to come out on top*, Allen & Unwin, 2007.
5. Lana Vidler, *Meals Men Love: How to catch a man in 3 courses*, Reldiv Group Pty Ltd, 2009.
6. John T. Molloy, *Why Men Marry Some Women and Not Others: The fascinating research that can land you the husband of your dreams*, Grand Central Publishing, 2004.
7. James Madison University study published in the journal *Sex Roles*, http://www.jmu.edu/, http://www.springerlink.com/content/d434653650281373/.
8. Louann Brizendine, *The Female Brain*, Broadway, 2006.
9. Steve Harvey, *Act Like a Lady, Think Like a Man*, Amistad, 2009.

10. John Gray, *Mars and Venus on a Date: A guide for navigating the 5 stages of dating to create a loving and lasting relationship*, Harper Collins, 1997.